Diabetes Desserts Cookbook

DECADENT CHOCOLATE TRUFFLES, PAGE 26

Diabetes *Desserts* Cookbook

CARB-SMART RECIPES TO SATISFY YOUR CRAVINGS

Ariel Warren,
RDN, CD, CDCES

RECIPES BY KATHERINE GREEN

R

ROCKRIDGE PRESS

For general information on our other products and services or to obtain technical support, please contact our Customer Care Department within the United States at (866) 744-2665, or outside the United States at (510) 253-0500.

Rockridge Press publishes its books in a variety of electronic and print formats. Some content that appears in print may not be available in electronic books, and vice versa.

TRADEMARKS: Rockridge Press and the Rockridge Press logo are trademarks or registered trademarks of Callisto Media Inc. and/or its affiliates, in the United States and other countries, and may not be used without written permission. All other trademarks are the property of their respective owners. Rockridge Press is not associated with any product or vendor mentioned in this book.

Interior and Cover Designer: Jennifer Hsu
Art Producer: Melissa Malinowsky
Editor: Rebecca Markley
Production Editor: Ashley Polikoff
Production Manager: Lanore Coloprisco

Photography © 2021 Laura Flippen, cover; © Johnny Autry, p. ii; © Olivia Brent, p. vi; © Darren Muir, pp. viii, 10, 100; © Hélène Dujardin, pp. 14, 38, 70, 92; © Andrew Purcell, pp. 18, 34; © Annie Martin, pp. 24, 48, 52; © Nadine Greeff, pp. 30, 44, 112; © Leigh Beisch, p. 60; © Kate Sears, p. 76; © Marija Vidal, p. 84; © Evi Abeler, pp. 116, 120.

Cover recipe: Chocolate-Hazelnut Crunch Cheesecake, page 90

Paperback ISBN: 978-1-638-07686-5
eBook ISBN: 978-1-638-78561-3
R0

To my loving husband, my beautiful children, my supportive parents and in-laws, and to all my friends who also have diabetes

Contents

Introduction

I was diagnosed with type 1 diabetes when I was four years old. Early on, I noticed how certain foods, such as frosted birthday cake and gooey s'mores, caused unruly blood sugar swings. Fast-forward many years later, and I had become increasingly aware of my diabetes and the different effects nutrition, exercise, and lifestyle habits had on my blood sugar. During that time, I also realized my unapologetic fondness for all things sweet and chocolate laden.

This all led me to become a registered dietitian nutritionist (RDN) and a Certified Diabetes Care and Education Specialist (CDCES). Today I speak at diabetes conferences, create online diabetes educational content, serve on the board for the Association of Diabetes Care and Education Specialists, write books and cookbooks for people with diabetes, and work with patients to help them eat a nutritious diet, manage their diabetes, and find balance and happiness throughout the process.

And what could be happier than dessert? My first memory of experimenting with healthier baking was when I was eight years old. I was whipping up some chocolate cupcakes with chocolate frosting. As I was sneaking in finger swipes of batter, I remember thinking, "Wow, the batter tastes like frosting, but it's not nearly as sugary." This inspired me to pour a fraction of the batter into the muffin tin, leaving the rest to be spread over the baked cupcakes as a frosting substitute.

As I frosted the last cupcake, I was beaming over my brilliance. Unfortunately, my family did not share my enthusiasm—especially since there were raw eggs and flour in my "frosting."

Don't worry: My early frosting hack is not included in this cookbook. After decades of experimenting (and acquiring a better understanding of food safety and basic cooking and baking principles), I've found there really isn't a reason why people with diabetes can't upgrade the ingredients in any given recipe to reduce the carbs and calories and increase the fiber and protein, all without compromising on taste, texture, and health. With that in mind, you'll find 62 of my all-time favorite desserts here, including fudgy brownies, cheesecake bars, and chewy chocolate chip cookies—all of which you can enjoy with peace of mind.

After all, life is meant to be enjoyed. With diabetes, you may feel at times that you have limited options, but it's more than possible to achieve great blood sugar control and still enjoy some little indulgences. Especially when chocolate is involved.

Chapter 1

The Diabetes Sweet Life

With this cookbook, you will learn how to swap ingredients, think outside the box, and make healthier versions of your favorites. You'll also get a review of the role of carbohydrates in diabetes and discover which alternative sweeteners can be helpful and which to avoid. Finally, I'll give you some easy tips to punch up the flavor of these desserts with healthy toppings that keep things carb savvy but also notch up the *wow factor* on flavor and overall presentation.

• Enjoying Dessert While Staying Healthy •

Part of the old-school advice for people diagnosed with diabetes was to cut out all desserts—really, anything with sugar—and carbohydrates. You know, *the good stuff.* However, more contemporary studies have shown that there isn't a one-diet-fits-all approach to managing diabetes. You can manage your diet based on your unique carbohydrate tolerance and personal preferences.

According to the American Diabetes Association, the dietary goal for someone with diabetes is to promote healthy eating patterns that emphasize nutrient-dense foods in appropriate portion sizes to improve overall health. By eating this way, you can better achieve body weight goals; attain individual glycemic, blood pressure, and lipid levels; and delay or prevent diabetes-related complications.

So if you love desserts, it's not about forever depriving yourself of chocolate and cheesecake. Instead, it's about finding the right amounts and making these goodies in a way that works for you and your health.

Each person has unique characteristics to be considered to optimize the way they manage their diabetes. By understanding *your* diabetes and working with your health-care team, you can recognize your unique boundaries; be educated on your type of diabetes, medication, and insulin needs; and create a personalized nutrition plan so you can enjoy life and achieve long-term success.

Then you can learn a couple of new tricks to make your favorite treats work with your diabetes. This little bit of extra effort will help you find balance, feel satisfied, and make mealtime more fun in the kitchen.

• The Role of Carbs and Sugar •

Diabetes-friendly desserts are not about cutting out all sugar and carbs entirely—although there are some ultra-low-carb recipes in this book. Instead, what makes a satisfying dessert safe for people with diabetes is its low net carb count—15 grams or fewer per serving.

There are three main types of carbohydrates: sugar, starch, and fiber. The important thing to keep in mind about them is that there are healthier carbs and not-as-healthy carbs in terms of how they affect your body and your blood glucose levels.

With the help of insulin, sugar travels into the cells of the body, where it can be used for energy. Insufficient insulin can cause elevated blood glucose levels, and because sugar is easy for the body to break down and use as energy, it raises blood sugar quickly, which can cause an even higher blood sugar spike for those with diabetes. This fast rise can come from refined sources of sugar, such as the granulated sugar found in a cookie, as well as the natural sugars in fruits, honey, and pure maple syrup. Although natural sugars are considered simple carbohydrates, in comparison to refined sugars, natural sugars are processed more slowly, which allows for more stable blood sugar control.

Starch or complex carbohydrates are found in foods such as potatoes, bread, rice, pasta, and cereals. Their molecular structure causes the body to take more energy and time to break them down into glucose. Starches raise blood sugar but more slowly than simple carbohydrates.

Fiber is the odd one out because it's a nondigestible carb, meaning the body can't break it down into absorbable energy, which is why fiber doesn't raise your blood sugar. It is your great blood sugar-stabilizing ally in diabetes. Fiber is what you use to calculate net carbs, the current gold standard in Diabetes 101 for determining how many carbs are in a serving of a particular food, which is often used to determine how to dose insulin or medication.

Net carbs are the number of carbs absorbed by the body that will raise blood sugar. To calculate net carbs in whole or packaged foods with nutrition labels, simply subtract the amount of fiber from the amount of total carbs. For example, a typical can of chickpeas has 20 grams of total carbs per ½-cup serving and 7 grams of fiber, so it has 13 grams of net carbs. To calculate net carbs in foods that contain sugar alcohols (any ingredient that ends with "itol," such as maltitol, sorbitol, and xylitol), subtract the fiber and part of the sugar alcohol. The amount to be subtracted depends on the sugar alcohol. But to be safe, it is often recommended to subtract half the grams of sugar alcohol used. So total carbs, minus the fiber, minus half the sugar alcohol.

One known exception to this rule is with erythritol, a sugar alcohol that has minimal (if any) impact, which is a big reason it is so popular with low-carb eaters. The carbs found in erythritol are known as non-impact carbs. Like fiber, non-impact carbs do not raise blood sugar, so they will not be counted in the net carbs for these dessert recipes.

Because everyone's diabetes management is different, you may find that you manage better using the total carbohydrate amount rather than net carbs—or somewhere in between. Do what works for you! If you are taking medication or insulin based on your carb count and you are used to NOT subtracting fiber, then do NOT subtract fiber with these recipes. All these recipes will give you the numbers for total carbohydrates, total fiber, and net carbs, so you have all the nutritional information you need to eat and properly dose what works for *you*. If there is a recipe that does not quite fit your management specifications, take it as an opportunity to get creative and make adaptations to give it your own delicious twist.

Sure, fluctuations with weight and blood sugar will undoubtedly occur, but the goal is for the general trend to stay steady, even when you need a treat. That is another reason I wrote this dessert book–so you can have a resource to satisfy your sweet tooth but still stay healthy.

Do Calories Count?

If you are trying to lose weight, these recipes can be a saving grace for when you are craving something sweet. Each of these recipes are low(er) in carbs, and many reduce total calories. But they were also created using healthier ingredients that naturally bulk up the protein and fiber content. Protein and fiber have also been found to naturally increase the feeling of fullness, and the fuller you feel, the better you can curb your appetite with fewer calories—and the easier it is to achieve a caloric deficit to reach your weight loss goals.

• Carb-Smart Flours •

There is a lot of hullabaloo concerning flour, for two reasons: gluten and all the carbs. Most sources say that gluten is safe for everyone except those who have celiac disease. However, if you have type 1 diabetes or have latent autoimmune diabetes as an adult, you have a 6 percent chance of also having celiac disease. This makes sense, since celiac disease is also an autoimmune condition. (Research does not show any increased risk of developing celiac disease if you have type 2 diabetes.)

Most of these recipes are naturally gluten-free or use wheat-based flours sparingly to reduce net carbs, since wheat flour is rather dense in net carbs. To be a more carb-savvy baker, here are other flours that are naturally lower in carbs. All-purpose (white) flour is included for comparison.

ALL-PURPOSE FLOUR

Taste: very mild with a subtle nuttiness

Types of desserts: biscuits, cookies, bread, donuts, crêpes, pancakes, waffles–basically every baked good

Net carbs per ¼ cup: 23 grams

Effect on blood sugar: high spike and quick rise due to high net carbs, with minimal amount of fiber, protein, and fat; use sparingly

ALMOND FLOUR

Taste: adds a sweet flavor, with a bit more nuttiness than all-purpose flour

Types of desserts: cookies, cakes, quick breads, and macarons

Net carbs per ¼ cup: 3 grams

Effect on blood sugar: minimal spike and slow rise due to low net carbs, with more protein and fat than all-purpose flour

COCONUT FLOUR

Taste: mild, sweet taste that has a fairly distinct coconut flavor

Types of desserts: moist baked goods such as cakes, brownies, and muffins

Net carbs per ¼ cup: 15 grams

Effect on blood sugar: mild spike and slow rise due to moderate net carbs, with more protein, fiber, and fat than all-purpose flour

GROUND FLAXSEED FLOUR

Taste: darker brown flaxseed has a nuttier and earthier flavor, while the lighter golden flaxseed is a bit milder all around

Types of desserts: flatbreads, or often used use to replace eggs in cookies, pancakes, muffins, and cakes

Net carbs per ¼ cup: 1 gram

Effect on blood sugar: minimal spike with a slow rise due to low net carbs, with more fiber, protein, and fat than all-purpose flour

Taste: a silky texture and a subtle nutty flavor that harmonizes well with ingredients such as honey, vanilla, cinnamon, and nutmeg

Types of desserts: pancakes, muffins, waffles, and quick breads

Net carbs per ¼ cup: 20 grams

Effect on blood sugar: high spike with a moderate rise due to higher net carbs, but more fiber and protein and slightly more fat than all-purpose flour

• Low-Carb Sweeteners •

What kind of sweetener you use to make your desserts—regular sugar or one of the alternatives listed here—should be moderated and tailored to your health goals and taste buds. In other words, if eating a certain sweetener makes you feel "off," there's always another sweetener to try. And if you don't like the taste of one, try another. Of course, if you prefer not to use sweeteners, you can always sweeten your desserts using natural sources such as fruits, honey, and pure maple syrup. Just make sure to dose your insulin or medication accordingly!

Although research is still being conducted to determine the long-term effects of eating even the more natural sweeteners, this cookbook uses a variety of ways to sweeten desserts: fruits, honey, pure maple syrup (not maple-*flavored* syrup), natural alternative sweeteners like stevia, and sugar alcohols like erythritol. In this section, I'm including only those sweeteners that remain stable at high temperatures without degrading or becoming toxic (important for baking!) and which have the least impact on blood sugar and overall health (with a few recommended limitations where needed).

NATURAL SWEETENERS

Natural sweeteners are made from concentrated components from edible plants. They have little to no impact on blood glucose or insulin levels.

Stevia (liquid or powdered): It tastes 200 to 300 times sweeter than sugar but can sometimes have a bitter, licorice-like, or even metallic aftertaste. For the healthiest version, look for "whole leaf stevia" on the label. Try it in ice creams, sorbets, and puddings. The recommended limit is 1.8 milligrams per pound of body weight per day.

Allulose (granulated): This is a natural sugar found in wheat, raisins, figs, and some other fruits. It's 30 percent less sweet than sugar with a similar mouthfeel and volume. It's great in cookies, cakes, bars, ice cream, cheesecakes, pies, frostings, preserves, syrups, sauces, and candies. The recommended limit is less than 0.4 grams per pound of body weight per day.

Monk Fruit (liquid or powdered): It's 100 to 250 times sweeter than sugar and can have an unusual or bitter aftertaste if it's not in a blend. Try the blended version in candies and sauces. There's no official recommended limit on this one.

SUGAR ALCOHOLS

These types of carbs are resistant to digestion, which means they raise blood glucose by only a fraction compared to regular sugar. In large quantities, they can cause digestive problems such as flatulence and bloating. I do not recommend mannitol, sorbitol, lactitol, maltitol, and isomalt because these sugar alcohols are considered more processed and are notorious for such unfavorable consequences. Also note that with any sugar alcohol, even the natural ones listed here, you may be more sensitive if you have never used them before.

Erythritol (granulated): It's 30 percent less sweet than sugar with a similar mouthfeel and volume. It has a cooling sensation on the tongue, particularly when used in large amounts. Use it in candy, chocolate, yogurt, fillings, preserves, and bars. Although it's a sugar alcohol, erythritol has not been found to have an impact on blood sugar or insulin levels. The recommended limit is 0.45 grams per pound of body weight per day.

Xylitol (powdered and granulated): Xylitol has the same sweetness level and volume as sugar. However, it causes a small rise in blood sugar due to partial digestion. Xylitol also has a similar cooling effect to erythritol and can be bitter in large quantities. It's best in desserts that do not rise, such as cookies, brownies, pies, and hard candies. The recommended limit is less than 30 grams per day.

BLENDS

There are some desserts where one alternative sweetener just can't get the job done. Think caramelization in cookies or that tender crumb in bars and cakes. This is why there are baking blends. Many baking blends will get their sweetness from stevia but use erythritol for the much-needed volume and to help with the moisture content. Just make sure to check that the ingredients come from pure

Sugar Substitutes to Avoid

Avoid aspartame, saccharin, acesulfame-K, and any other nonnutritive sweeteners produced using synthetic methods. Each artificial sweetener is broken down in different regions in the gut, and all have been found to have varying effects depending on factors such as age, gender, and even ethnicity. Though many studies have been conducted using mice, the information, even if it is lacking direct human evidence, is alarming.

At worst, artificial sweeteners stimulate appetite, leading to weight gain; damage your gut microbiome; increase your risk of developing metabolic and cardiovascular disease; and increase inflammation. At best, using artificial sweeteners has little to no short- or long-term effects, allowing you to satisfy your sweet tooth without problems when consumed within their recommended safe doses. Overall, evidence suggests that it's best to moderate or eliminate artificial sweeteners altogether to stay on the safer side, especially when there are other healthier and less questionable options to satisfy your craving for something sweet.

sources and avoid sweeteners or fillers that may spike blood sugar or have been found to cause other adverse effects on health, such as maltodextrin, dextrose, and isomaltooligosaccharides (IMO).

• Flavors and Fats •

These diabetes-friendly recipes are all about swapping out certain ingredients to give classic desserts a total nutrient-boosting, carb-lowering makeover. For example, by simply swapping out some of the butter in a recipe for pureed avocado, almond butter, or pumpkin puree, you can reduce saturated fat, eliminate cholesterol, and reduce sodium while upping the vitamin, mineral, fiber, and protein load–all of which are vital for better health, improved blood sugar control, and helping you feel fuller (which helps reduce total calorie intake). The following is a list of my favorite ingredient swaps for fats and calories that you will find throughout this cookbook.

UNSWEETENED APPLESAUCE

Net carbs for ½ cup: 12 grams

Nutrition: lowers fat and calories; adds fiber and vitamin C

Types of desserts: high-moisture cookies, cakes, quick breads like banana and zucchini bread

LOW-FAT PLAIN GREEK YOGURT

Net carbs for ½ cup: 5 grams

Nutrition: lowers fat and calories; adds protein and calcium

Types of desserts: mousses, cheesecakes, frozen yogurt, ice cream, yogurt tarts, frosting glaze, frozen yogurt fruit bites and barks, creamy ice pops, crème brûlée, parfaits

NUT BUTTERS

Net carbs for ½ cup: 16 grams for peanut butter; 12 grams for almond butter

Nutrition: healthier monounsaturated fats; adds protein, fiber, vitamins B_6 and E, magnesium, copper, and calcium

Types of desserts: bars, cookies, fudges, sauces, ice cream, quick breads, baked donuts, muffins

PUMPKIN PUREE

Net carbs for ½ cup: 7 grams

Nutrition: lowers fat and calories; adds fiber, some protein, and vitamin C; is a fantastic source of beta-carotene

Types of desserts: mousse, pies, pudding, muffins, cookies, bars, moist breads

PUREED AVOCADO

Net carbs for ½ cup: 1 gram

Nutrition: healthier monounsaturated fats; adds fiber, protein, and vitamins K, C, B_3, and B_5

Types of desserts: fudge, brownies, chocolate mousse and puddings, truffles, tarts, ice cream, creamy ice pops, buttercream frosting, bars, baked donuts, cookies

VIRGIN COCONUT OIL

Net carbs for ½ cup: 0 grams

Nutrition: healthier saturated fats (although higher in saturated fat than butter, the type of saturated fat in coconut oil, MCT lauric acid, has been found to increase healthy HDL cholesterol)

Types of desserts: cookies, bars, cakes, crisps, crumbles, crusts, scones, granola, breads, baked donuts

• Healthy Garnishes •

Dessert should entice and delight, and the eyes are the first to notice. With these recipes, I'm all about the nutrient content while keeping the carbs low, but I love adding a dust, sprinkle, or drizzle of a healthy topping to add a little extra *oomph* without breaking the net carb bank. (In addition to these ideas, you will find five recipes for tasty toppings in chapter 7.)

Unsweetened Coconut Flakes: To add a slightly sweet, nutty taste, press them into drop cookies or sprinkle them on brownies and parfaits.

Powdered Natural Sweetener: A substitute for confectioners' sugar, a powdered natural sweetener (such as erythritol) is wonderful for dusting baked goods such as candies, fudge, sweet breads, brownies, cookies, and baked donuts. Or churn it into a frosting for shortbread cookies, moist cakes, and sweet breads.

Cinnamon: Mix with some granulated natural sweetener to accent spice cookies, snickerdoodles, apple and pumpkin tarts, or anything that needs a touch more flavor.

Cacao Nibs: Nibs are pieces of crushed cacao beans that boost nutrition by providing extra protein, fiber, magnesium, and healthy fats. Some are roasted; unroasted ones are called raw cacao nibs. Mix them into batters, sprinkle them on top of freshly baked cookies or bars, or toss them into a fruit salad to add a bit of chocolaty, earthy, nutty crunch.

Unsweetened Cocoa or Cacao Powder: Adds a deep chocolate flavor. Cacao powder is less processed, which boosts the nutrition, but it can have a more bitter taste. Sift either powder with a tea strainer over baked goods to add elegance and intensify the chocolate experience.

Chopped Nuts: Add as a topping or mix them into the batter or dough of cookies, cakes, bars, muffins, and pastries for added crunch and texture. As a bonus, nuts are also a good source of protein and healthy fat. To intensify the flavor, I highly recommend toasting the nuts first.

• About the Recipes •

With diabetes-friendly desserts, blood sugar control is a top priority. That's why every recipe breaks down the important nutritional information for total carbohydrates, fiber, and net carbs. Both total and net carbs are provided just in case you do better using one over the other for dosing medication and insulin.

In each recipe, you will be directed to sweeten the treat using honey, fruit, maple syrup, or an alternative sweetener in the form of brown, granulated, or powdered "sweetener of choice." I made the recipes this way so that you can choose the sweeteners and blends that best suit your taste and health needs.

You will also see the ingredient "milk of choice" used throughout for greater flexibility in the kitchen. You can use an unsweetened nut milk, coconut milk, oat milk, or even dairy milk. Just know that the nutritional information was calculated using unsweetened nut milk, which has about 30 calories, 1 gram of carbs, and 1 gram of protein in 1 cup. (For comparison, low-fat cow's milk has about 110 calories, 12 grams of carbs, and 8 grams of protein per cup.)

If you are more sensitive with your blood sugar and have a lower carb tolerance, understand that you need to tailor the frequency and choice of desserts to suit you. Once you learn when you can indulge and what you can eat and still keep within your management goals, take the time to treat yourself. Then spread the joy by sharing your favorite cookie, pie, or brownie recipe with your friends and family. Their blood sugar will thank you, too!

LIME–BERRY COCONUT ICE POPS, PAGE 21

Chapter 2
Light Treats

Raspberry-Coconut Bliss Balls

MAKES 12 BALLS

PREP TIME: 10 minutes, plus 15 minutes to soak

¼ cup pitted dates (about 2 ounces)

½ cup almond flour

¾ cup unsweetened shredded coconut, divided

½ cup frozen raspberries

Sweetened naturally with dates, these delightful bites are loaded with healthy fats, natural sweetness, fiber, and oh-so-much delicious flavor. Coconut and raspberry are an unlikely pair, but they are definitely a harmonious blend, especially if you are a fan of super simple bite-size treats.

1. Put the dates in a small bowl and cover with hot water. Let sit for 15 minutes to soften. Drain.

2. To make the dough, put the flour, ½ cup of shredded coconut, the raspberries, and dates in a food processor. Process until smooth.

3. Roll the dough into 12 (1-inch) balls.

4. Put the remaining ¼ cup of shredded coconut in a small bowl, and roll the balls in it to coat.

Make it last: Store the balls in an airtight container in the refrigerator for up to 4 days.

PER SERVING (2 BALLS): *Calories: 130; Total fat: 11g; Total carbohydrates: 9g; Fiber: 3g; Net carbs: 6g; Added sugar: 0g; Protein: 3g*

Berry Yogurt Frozen Bites

MAKES 12 BITES

PREP TIME: 10 minutes, plus 4 hours to freeze

1½ cups plain low-fat Greek yogurt

¼ cup milk of choice

2 tablespoons granulated sweetener of choice

1 teaspoon vanilla extract

1 cup raspberries

This is a refreshing treat on a hot day, and you can use up any extra fruit you may already have on hand. Raspberries are my absolute favorite because they are super low in net carbohydrates yet high in antioxidants and dietary fiber. However, strawberries, blackberries, or blueberries are wonderful, too. If you want to dress this recipe up more and add extra protein and healthy fat, try sprinkling on crushed cacao nibs or flax, hemp, or chia seeds. You can also add a subtle pop of flavor by topping the bites with fresh thyme leaves or grated lemon or lime zest. If you prefer a more natural sweetener, you can easily use 1 teaspoon of honey or skip the sweetener altogether and rely on the natural sweetness from the berries. Just remember that 1 teaspoon of honey equals an extra 5 grams of carbs.

1. In a small bowl, combine the yogurt, milk, sweetener, and vanilla. Mix well.

2. Sprinkle the raspberries evenly over an ice cube tray or other mold with small sections.

3. Pour the yogurt mixture over the berries to fill the ice cube tray. Freeze for at least 4 hours or overnight.

4. Once frozen, remove the bites from the container and store in the freezer.

Make it last: Store the bites in an airtight container in the freezer for up to 3 months.

PER SERVING (4 BITES): *Calories: 123; Total fat: 3g; Total carbohydrates: 12g; Fiber: 3g; Net carbs: 9g; Added sugar: 0g; Protein: 13g*

Cheesecake-Stuffed Strawberries

SERVES 4

PREP TIME: 15 minutes

12 large strawberries

4 ounces low-fat cream cheese, at room temperature

1 tablespoon pure maple syrup or honey

1 teaspoon vanilla extract

2 tablespoons crushed almonds (optional)

This is a lovely dessert to serve to guests, since these stuffed strawberries look rather elegant on a platter. For added flair, use a piping bag or simply put the filling in a resealable plastic bag. Cut a small piece from a bottom corner, and pipe the filling into the strawberries. To lower the carbs even more, use 1 tablespoon of a granulated sweetener of choice in place of the maple syrup—and the crushed almonds are optional.

1. Using a paring knife, cut the tops off the strawberries and hollow them out to make a hole for the filling.

2. To make the filling, in a medium bowl using a handheld electric mixer, beat together the cream cheese, maple syrup, and vanilla on medium speed until smooth. Turn off the mixer.

3. Spoon or pipe the filling into the strawberries, and arrange them on a tray.

4. Sprinkle with the crushed almonds (if using).

Make it last: Store the stuffed strawberries in an airtight container in the refrigerator for up to 3 days.

PER SERVING (3 STRAWBERRIES): *Calories: 110; Total fat: 4.5g; Total carbohydrates: 14g; Fiber: 2g; Net carbs: 12g; Added sugar: 4g; Protein: 3g*

Melon-Berry Granita

SERVES 8

PREP TIME: 5 minutes, plus 3 hours to freeze

2 cups chopped cantaloupe

2 cups fresh or frozen mixed berries, such as blackberries, blueberries, strawberries, or raspberries

1 cup water

2 tablespoons honey

1 teaspoon fresh thyme leaves

Granita is a semi-frozen treat made from fruit, sugar, and water, and in this version, cantaloupe and berries provide a punch of flavor. Sweetened naturally with honey and accented with thyme, this is perfect for a hot day when you want a grown-up healthy treat. If desired, use 2 tablespoons of granulated sweetener of choice in place of the honey to lower the net carbs to 7 grams per serving (8 grams total carbohydrates and 1 gram of fiber).

1. Put the cantaloupe, berries, water, honey, and thyme in a blender. Blend until smooth. Transfer to a bowl. Freeze the mixture for about 2 hours.

2. Remove the bowl from the freezer, and using a fork, break the mixture up into ice granules.

3. Return the bowl to the freezer for 1 hour. Break up again with a fork, then serve.

Make it last: Freeze the granita for up to 5 days in an airtight container. Use a fork to break the granita into granules before serving.

PER SERVING: *Calories: 60; Total fat: 0g; Total carbohydrates: 15g; Fiber: 2g; Net carbs: 13g; Added sugar: 6g; Protein: 1g*

Lime-Berry Coconut Ice Pops

SERVES 6

PREP TIME: 5 minutes,
plus 6 hours to freeze

1 cup sliced strawberries

½ cup blueberries

2 tablespoons honey

1 (14-ounce) can light
coconut milk

¼ cup water

Grated zest and juice
of 1 lime

Ice pops are a wonderful light dessert, perfect for a hot day or when you're feeling young at heart. These simple fruity frozen pops require just a handful of ingredients, and you can use any fresh or frozen berries you have on hand. If you use firmer berries like strawberries or blackberries or if you just like a smoother texture, blend the fruit and coconut milk in a blender before mixing in the remaining ingredients. If desired, use 2 tablespoons of granulated sweetener of choice in place of the honey to lower the net carbs to 2 grams per serving (4 grams total carbohydrates and 2 grams of fiber).

1. In a large bowl, combine the strawberries, blueberries, and honey. Mix well.

2. Stir in the coconut milk, water, and lime zest and juice. Mix well.

3. Pour the mixture into 6 ice pop molds or small paper cups. Insert sticks and freeze for 6 hours, or until solid.

4. To serve, run the ice pop molds or cups under warm water for a few seconds to remove the pops.

Make it last: Store the ice pops in an airtight container in the freezer for up to 1 month.

PER SERVING: *Calories: 60; Total fat: 2.5g; Total carbohydrates: 11g; Fiber: 2g; Net carbs: 9g; Added sugar: 6g; Protein: 0g*

Chocolate-Almond Fudge

MAKES 8 PIECES

PREP TIME: 10 minutes,
plus 2 hours to chill

1 cup no-sugar-added
chocolate chips

1 tablespoon
coconut oil

2 tablespoons natural
peanut butter

½ cup coarsely chopped
roasted almonds

This Chocolate-Almond Fudge is one of my favorites because it literally takes just a few minutes to prepare and contains only four ingredients, making it about as simple as can be. A small 4-by-4-inch baking dish is perfect for making this, but if you don't have one, use a parchment paper-lined storage container of similar size instead. Once the fudge is solid, lift it out of the dish using the paper, and cut it into squares to serve.

1. Line a 4-inch square baking dish with parchment paper, with some paper overhanging the sides.

2. In a glass bowl, combine the chocolate chips and oil. Microwave in 30-second intervals, stirring in between each interval, until melted.

3. Mix in the peanut butter and stir well.

4. Pour the mixture into the prepared dish, spreading it out to fill the bottom.

5. Sprinkle with the almonds, and press them down into the chocolate. Refrigerate the fudge for 2 hours to set.

6. Lift the fudge out of the dish, and cut into 8 pieces.

Make it last: Store the fudge in an airtight container for up to 2 weeks in the refrigerator.

PER SERVING: *Calories: 170; Total fat: 13g; Total carbohydrates: 13g; Fiber: 7g; Net carbs: 6g; Added sugar: 0g; Protein: 5g*

Salted Peanut Butter Fudge

MAKES 8 PIECES

PREP TIME: 10 minutes, plus 2 hours to chill

½ cup creamy natural peanut butter

½ cup unsweetened coconut flakes

¼ cup coconut oil, melted

2 tablespoons pure maple syrup

1 teaspoon vanilla extract

½ cup no-sugar-added chocolate chips

¼ teaspoon coarse sea salt

This sweet and savory dessert is another quickie, and it delivers the full flavor and chewy texture of fudgy goodness. Coconut oil, chocolate, and coconut flakes keep the fudge firm at room temperature, but keep in mind that if it's hot enough in your kitchen to make your coconut oil liquid at room temperature, you will want to keep these in the refrigerator until you're ready to serve.

1. Line a 4-inch square baking dish with parchment paper, with some paper overhanging the sides.

2. In a medium bowl, combine the peanut butter, coconut flakes, oil, maple syrup, and vanilla. Mix well.

3. Put the chocolate chips in a small glass bowl and microwave in 30-second intervals, stirring in between each interval, until melted.

4. Pour the melted chocolate into the peanut butter mixture and swirl without thoroughly mixing everything together. Transfer to the prepared dish.

5. Sprinkle the salt evenly over the top. Refrigerate the fudge for at least 2 hours, or until solid.

6. Lift the fudge out of the dish, and cut into 8 pieces. Refrigerate until you are ready to serve.

Make it last: Store the fudge in an airtight container for up to 2 weeks in the refrigerator.

PER SERVING: *Calories: 220; Total fat: 12g; Total carbohydrates: 13g; Fiber: 4g; Net carbs: 9g; Added sugar: 3g; Protein: 5g*

No-Bake Cookie Dough Truffles

MAKES 12 TRUFFLES

PREP TIME: 10 minutes, plus 1 hour to freeze

1½ cups almond flour

½ cup coconut flour

½ cup powdered sweetener of choice

¼ teaspoon salt

6 tablespoons coconut oil, melted

1 teaspoon vanilla extract

½ cup no-sugar-added chocolate chips

½ cup crushed walnuts

No-bake truffles are a perfect treat for any occasion, and these will not disappoint. Using a mixture of almond and coconut flour creates a delicious little truffle treat that is reminiscent of eating cookie dough from the bowl. The chopped nuts are a lovely addition (you can use walnuts as I've done here, almonds, or another nut of choice, if desired), or if you like, dip the truffles in a little melted chocolate to coat one side for a gourmet look.

1. To make the dough, in a bowl, stir together the almond flour, coconut flour, sweetener, and salt.

2. Stir in the oil and vanilla, then mix in the chocolate chips.

3. Scoop out tablespoon-size pieces of the dough, and using your hands, shape into balls. Place on a plate, and repeat with the remaining dough to make 12 truffles.

4. Put the walnuts in a small bowl. Roll the truffles in the walnuts and return to the plate. Freeze for 1 hour to harden, then serve.

Make it last: Store the truffles in an airtight container in the refrigerator for up to 1 week.

PER SERVING: *Calories: 170; Total fat: 16g, Total carbohydrates: 9g, Fiber: 5g, Net carbs: 4g, Added Sugar: 0g, Protein: 4g*

Decadent Chocolate Truffles

MAKES 12 TRUFFLES

PREP TIME: 15 minutes, plus 30 minutes to chill

4 ounces unsweetened chocolate, coarsely chopped

1 tablespoon coconut oil

¼ cup coconut cream

¼ cup granulated sweetener of choice

1 teaspoon vanilla extract

1 tablespoon unsweetened cocoa powder

1 tablespoon unsweetened shredded coconut

My family *loves* making truffles because it is so fun to let everyone choose their own toppings. My personal favorite is toasted coconut flakes. YUMMY! If you haven't already, you need to try toasting coconut flakes and adding them to any chocolate recipe. Try your favorite standard toppings, or experiment with something new. Some of my favorites are chopped nuts, seeds, and even dried fruit. However, if you mind stickiness, wear some disposable gloves before mixing.

1. In a small microwave-safe bowl, combine the chocolate and oil. Microwave on high in 30-second intervals, stirring in between each interval, until melted.

2. Stir in the coconut cream, then microwave for about 20 seconds to heat through. Mix well.

3. Stir in the sweetener and vanilla. Mix well. Transfer the bowl to the freezer for 30 minutes to solidify the mixture.

4. Scoop out 2 teaspoon-size pieces of dough, and using your hands, shape into balls. Place on a plate.

5. Put the cocoa powder in one small bowl and the shredded coconut in another. Roll half of the truffles in the cocoa powder and the remaining half in the coconut. Serve immediately.

Make it last: Store the truffles in an airtight container in the refrigerator for up to 4 days.

PER SERVING (2 TRUFFLES): *Calories: 180; Total fat: 14g; Total carbohydrates: 7g; Fiber: 4g; Net carbs: 3g; Added sugar: 0g; Protein: 3g*

Lime, Mint, and Orange Yogurt Parfait

SERVES 4

PREP TIME: 10 minutes

2 cups plain low-fat Greek yogurt

Grated zest and juice of 1 lime

2 tablespoons granulated sweetener of choice

1 (8-ounce) can mandarin oranges in juice, drained

4 or 5 fresh mint leaves, sliced

Parfaits are an easy dessert that can be completely customized to anyone's taste. This simple version uses a mix of orange, lime, and mint, but you can use any combination of fruit and citrus juice. Grapefruit, blackberries, blueberries, and strawberries are all delightful substitutes for the mandarin oranges.

1. In a large bowl, mix together the yogurt, lime zest and juice, and sweetener.

2. Put a few segments of oranges into each of 4 small glasses.

3. Divide the yogurt mixture among the glasses and top with the remaining orange slices.

4. Sprinkle the mint leaves over the top of the parfaits.

Make it last: Store the parfaits covered in the refrigerator for up to 3 days.

PER SERVING: *Calories: 110; Total fat: 2.5g; Total carbohydrates: 6g; Fiber: 1g; Net carbs: 5g; Added sugar: 0g; Protein: 13g*

Ambrosia Salad

SERVES 6

PREP TIME: 10 minutes,
plus 1 hour to chill

1 cup sliced fresh
strawberries

1 cup fresh blueberries

1 cup fresh blackberries

¼ cup unsweetened
coconut flakes

¾ cup Whipped Coconut
Cream (page 121)

¼ cup chopped walnuts

This classic dessert salad gets a berry makeover that's bursting with the antioxidant-rich trio of strawberries, blackberries, and blueberries. Coconut flakes and Whipped Coconut Cream (page 121) combine to give it a luxurious feel without the typical dairy. Walnuts add a bit of crunch and an extra nutritional boost of omega-3 fatty acids.

1. In a large bowl, combine the strawberries, blueberries, blackberries, and coconut flakes.

2. Fold in the coconut cream to combine. Chill for at least 1 hour.

3. Top with the walnuts to serve.

Make it last: Store the salad in an airtight container in the refrigerator for up to 2 days.

PER SERVING: *Calories: 180; Total fat: 15g; Total carbohydrates: 11g; Fiber: 3g; Net carbs: 8g; Added sugar: 0g; Protein: 2g*

Roasted Plums with Yogurt

SERVES 4

PREP TIME: 10 minutes

COOK TIME: 20 minutes

4 large (2⅛-inch) firm plums, sliced

1 tablespoon pure maple syrup

1 (1-inch) piece fresh ginger, grated

¼ teaspoon ground cinnamon

Grated zest of 1 lime

1 cup plain low-fat Greek yogurt or coconut yogurt

Plums are dressed up here with ginger and cinnamon, two spices that will make your kitchen smell lovely as they cook. Roasting is an easy way to caramelize the natural sugars in stone fruit–make this recipe with nectarines or peaches for equal deliciousness. If you prefer, use 10 liquid stevia drops and 2 teaspoons of water in place of the maple syrup. This will lower the net carbs to 10 grams per serving (12 grams total carbohydrates and 2 grams of fiber).

1. Preheat the oven to 375°F. Line a baking sheet with parchment paper.

2. In a large bowl, combine the plums, maple syrup, ginger, cinnamon, and lime zest.

3. Arrange the plum slices in a single layer on the prepared baking sheet.

4. Transfer the baking sheet to the oven and roast for 15 to 20 minutes, or until the plums are tender and the sugars are slightly caramelized. Remove from the oven.

5. Top each serving with ¼ cup of yogurt.

Make it last: Store the roasted plums in an airtight container for up to 3 days in the refrigerator. Warm in the microwave or serve cold.

PER SERVING (1 PLUM): *Calories: 90; Total fat: 1.5g; Total carbohydrates: 14g; Fiber: 1g; Net carbs: 13g; Added sugar: 3g; Protein: 7g*

CHOCOLATE CHIP COOKIES, PAGE 46

Chapter 3
Cookies

No-Bake Coconut Cookies

MAKES 12 COOKIES

PREP TIME: 10 minutes,
plus 30 minutes to chill

**2 cups shredded
unsweetened coconut**

¼ cup almond flour

¼ cup coconut oil, melted

¼ cup pure maple syrup

These cookies are no-bake superstars that come together in just minutes. Maple syrup naturally sweetens these delicious cookies, which are loaded with healthy fats from the coconut. For a more rustic-looking cookie, be sure to use shredded unsweetened coconut, although flakes will work well, too.

1. In a large bowl, mix together the shredded coconut, flour, oil, and maple syrup.

2. Using your hands, press the mixture into heaping tablespoon-size balls.

3. Place the balls on a baking sheet. Using your palm, press them into flattened discs. Refrigerate for 30 minutes, or until firm.

Make it last: Store the cookies in an airtight container in the refrigerator for up to 1 week, or freeze for up to 6 months.

PER SERVING (1 COOKIE): *Calories: 160; Total fat: 14g; Total carbohydrates: 8g; Fiber: 2g; Net carbs: 6g; Added sugar: 4g; Protein: 1g*

Ginger Snaps

MAKES 12 COOKIES

PREP TIME: 10 minutes

COOK TIME: 15 minutes

¼ cup coconut oil, melted

¼ cup pure maple syrup

1 large egg

2 tablespoons water

2½ cups almond flour

2 teaspoons
  ground ginger

1 teaspoon ground
  cinnamon

1 teaspoon baking soda

¼ teaspoon salt

Ginger has a peppery warming flavor that is delicious in cookies. Every year during the holidays, we make ginger cookies and gingerbread houses, but ginger snaps are a cookie that can be enjoyed any time. In addition to tasting delicious, ginger helps stimulate digestion and boost circulation, making it a healthy addition to your desserts. This version uses almond flour to achieve a low-carb cookie that tastes amazing.

1. Preheat the oven to 325°F. Line a baking sheet with parchment paper.

2. In a large bowl, whisk together the oil, maple syrup, egg, and water.

3. Add the flour, ginger, cinnamon, baking soda, and salt. Stir to mix well.

4. Scoop heaping tablespoon-size balls about 2 inches apart onto the prepared baking sheet. Using the palm of your hand, gently press the balls to flatten into cookies.

5. Transfer the baking sheet to the oven and bake for 12 to 14 minutes, or until the cookies have lightly browned. Remove from the oven.

Make it last: Store the cookies in an airtight container for up to 1 week.

PER SERVING (1 COOKIE): *Calories: 130; Total fat: 11g; Total carbohydrates: 7g; Fiber: 2g; Net carbs: 5g; Added sugar: 4g; Protein: 3g*

Berry Thumbprint Cookies

MAKES 16 COOKIES

PREP TIME: 15 minutes

COOK TIME: 15 minutes

¼ cup Berry Fruit Sauce
  (page 118)

1½ teaspoons chia seeds

1¾ cups almond flour

½ cup granulated
  sweetener of choice

½ cup coconut oil

2 large eggs

1 teaspoon vanilla extract

These cookies were one of my favorites as a kid, and this recipe is just as fun to make as it is to enjoy. Use your thumbprint to shape the cup for this simple and quick jam, created using the Berry Fruit Sauce (page 118) combined with chia seeds. If you don't want to make the jam, just substitute any no-sugar-added jam you have on hand and leave out the chia seeds.

1. Preheat the oven to 325°F. Line a baking sheet with parchment paper.

2. To make the jam, in a small bowl, mix together the berry fruit sauce and chia seeds. Let sit for 10 minutes, or until thickened.

3. In a large bowl, combine the flour, sweetener, and oil. Add the eggs and vanilla. Mix well.

4. Scoop 1-inch balls about 2 inches apart onto the prepared baking sheet.

5. Transfer the baking sheet to the oven and bake for 5 minutes.

6. Remove the baking sheet from the oven, leaving the oven on. Using your thumb, press the cookies gently on top to make an indent.

7. Spoon a small amount of the jam into each indent.

8. Return the baking sheet to the oven and bake for 8 to 10 minutes, or until the cookies have lightly browned. Remove from the oven. Let cool completely before removing from the sheet.

PER SERVING (1 COOKIE): *Calories: 130; Total fat: 13g; Total carbohydrates: 4g; Fiber: 2g; Net carbs: 2g; Added sugar: 0g; Protein: 3g*

Glazed Sugar Cookies

MAKES 24 COOKIES

PREP TIME: 10 minutes, plus 30 minutes to chill

COOK TIME: 15 minutes

1½ cups almond flour

½ cup granulated sweetener of choice

¼ cup coconut flour

Pinch salt

½ cup coconut oil

1 large egg

2 teaspoons vanilla extract, divided

½ cup powdered sweetener of choice

1 tablespoon coconut cream

I have a special place in my heart for glazed sugar cookies. I have so many memories of decorating them as holiday treats and many "just because" moments making them in the kitchen with my kids. With this recipe, a mixture of almond flour and coconut flour gives these cookies a similar texture to the original but without all the carbs. If you prefer to use cookie cutter shapes, you can shape the dough into a round disc, chill, and roll the dough out on a piece of parchment paper to ¼-inch thickness. If you like, add a few drops of food coloring to the frosting to make it more festive.

1. In a large bowl, combine the almond flour, granulated sweetener, coconut flour, and salt.

2. Add the oil, egg, and 1 teaspoon of vanilla. Using a handheld electric mixer, mix on medium speed until the dough begins to clump together. Turn off the mixer.

3. Shape the dough into a log about 1½ inches in diameter and 8 inches long, and wrap with plastic wrap. Refrigerate for at least 30 minutes, or until firm. At this point, the dough can be refrigerated for up to 2 days.

4. When you're ready to bake, preheat the oven to 325°F. Line a baking sheet with parchment paper.

5. Cut the cookie dough log into generous ¼-inch-thick rounds.

6. Place the cookies on the prepared baking sheet.

7. Transfer the baking sheet to the oven and bake for 12 to 15 minutes, or until the cookies have just lightly browned. Remove from the oven. Let rest on the sheet for about 10 minutes, then transfer to a wire rack until completely cool.

8. In a small bowl, combine the powdered sweetener, coconut cream, and remaining 1 teaspoon of vanilla. Mix until the sweetener has dissolved, adding a little water or almond milk as needed to create a spreadable icing.

9. Spread the icing onto the cooled cookies and serve.

Make it last: Store the cookies for up to 5 days in an airtight container.

PER SERVING (2 COOKIES): *Calories: 180; Total fat: 16g; Total carbohydrates: 5g; Fiber: 2g; Net carbs: 3g; Added sugar: 0g; Protein: 3g*

Snowball Cookies

MAKES 16 COOKIES

PREP TIME: 15 minutes

COOK TIME: 15 minutes

½ cup coconut oil, melted

½ cup granulated sweetener of choice

2 large eggs

1 teaspoon vanilla extract

2 cups almond flour

Pinch salt

¼ cup chopped walnuts

¼ cup powdered sweetener of choice

Snowball cookies are popular around the holidays, and you won't have to miss out with this version. Be sure to roll them in the powdered sweetener before they have completely cooled so the powder will stick to the surface–but also keep in mind that all gluten-free cookies need to rest for at least a few minutes after baking to firm up.

1. Preheat the oven to 350°F. Line a baking sheet with parchment paper.

2. To make the dough, in a large bowl, combine the oil, granulated sweetener, eggs, and vanilla. Mix well to combine.

3. Stir in the flour, salt, and walnuts, and mix until the dough holds together.

4. Scoop teaspoon-size balls about 1 inch apart onto the prepared baking sheet.

5. Transfer the baking sheet to the oven and bake for 13 to 16 minutes, or until the cookies have lightly browned. Remove from the oven. Let cool on the sheet for 5 minutes.

6. Put the powdered sweetener in a small bowl. Gently roll the warm cookies in the powdered sweetener, shaking off the excess. Set aside to completely cool.

Make it last: Store the cookies in an airtight container for up to 5 days.

PER SERVING (1 COOKIE): *Calories: 99 calories; Total fat: 10g, Total carbohydrates: 2g, Fiber: 1g, Net carbs: 1g, Added sugar: 0g: Protein: 2g*

Oatmeal-Coconut Cookies

MAKES 24 COOKIES

PREP TIME: 15 minutes

COOK TIME: 10 minutes

1 cup almond flour

1 cup old-fashioned oatmeal

1 cup shredded unsweetened coconut

1 teaspoon ground cinnamon

1 teaspoon baking powder

¼ teaspoon salt

5 tablespoons coconut oil, at room temperature

½ cup granulated sweetener of choice

2 large eggs

2 teaspoons vanilla extract

Using a combination of almond flour, oatmeal, and coconut, these cookies have a most delectable chewy texture and slightly nutty flavor. The texture is close to a classic oatmeal cookie, and the mix of coconut and sweetener gives the perfect amount of sweetness. Ground cinnamon is the impeccable match for oatmeal cookies since it gives them a subtle sweet and warm flavor. And as an added bonus, cinnamon helps increase insulin sensitivity, which helps improve blood sugar control.

1. Preheat the oven to 350°F. Line a baking sheet with parchment paper.

2. In a medium bowl, mix together the flour, oatmeal, coconut, cinnamon, baking powder, and salt.

3. In a large bowl using a handheld electric mixer, cream the oil with the sweetener on high speed, scraping down the sides of the bowl.

4. Add the eggs and vanilla. Mix well.

5. Reduce the speed to low. Add the flour mixture and mix until combined. Turn off the mixer.

6. Scoop tablespoon-size balls about 2 inches apart onto the prepared baking sheet. Using the palm of your hand, gently press the balls to flatten into cookies about ¼ inch thick.

7. Transfer the baking sheet to the oven and bake for 10 to 12 minutes, or until the cookies are just starting to brown. Remove from the oven. Let cool on the sheet for 5 minutes, then transfer to a wire rack to fully cool.

Make it last: Store the cookies in an airtight container for up to 5 days.

PER SERVING (2 COOKIES): *Calories: 180; Total fat: 15g; Total carbohydrates: 8g; Fiber: 3g; Net carbs: 5g; Added sugar: 1g; Protein: 4g*

Snickerdoodle Cookies

MAKES 24 COOKIES

PREP TIME: 10 minutes

COOK TIME: 15 minutes

2 cups almond flour

⅓ cup granulated sweetener of choice, plus 2 tablespoons

2 teaspoons ground cinnamon, divided

½ teaspoon baking powder

6 tablespoons coconut oil

1 large egg

1 teaspoon vanilla extract

This childhood favorite comes with a cinnamon-sugar coating and a soft and chewy inside, just like the original, but with only 2 grams net carbs per serving. Be sure to flatten the cookies before baking, since they will not spread naturally on their own.

1. Preheat the oven to 350°F. Line a baking sheet with parchment paper.

2. In a large bowl, mix together the flour, ⅓ cup of sweetener, 1 teaspoon of cinnamon, and the baking powder.

3. In a small bowl, mix together the oil, egg, and vanilla.

4. Mix the wet ingredients with the dry ingredients.

5. In another small bowl, mix together the remaining 2 tablespoons of sweetener and 1 teaspoon of cinnamon.

6. Scoop the dough into heaping tablespoon-size pieces and roll into balls.

7. Roll the balls in the cinnamon-sweetener mixture.

8. Place the balls about 1 inch apart on the prepared baking sheet. Using the palm of your hand, gently press the balls to flatten into cookies.

9. Transfer the baking sheet to the oven and bake for 12 to 15 minutes, or until the cookies have lightly browned. Remove from the oven. Let cool on the sheet.

Make it last: Store the cookies in an airtight container for up to 3 days.

PER SERVING (2 COOKIES): *Calories: 170; Total fat: 15g; Total carbohydrates: 4g; Fiber: 2g; Net carbs: 2g; Added sugar: 0g; Protein: 4g*

Cowboy Cookies

MAKES 30 COOKIES

PREP TIME: 10 minutes

COOK TIME: 10 minutes

1 cup almond flour

1 cup unsweetened shredded coconut

½ cup old-fashioned oats

½ cup granulated sweetener of choice

1 teaspoon baking powder

1 teaspoon ground cinnamon

¼ teaspoon salt

¼ cup coconut oil, melted

2 large eggs

1 teaspoon vanilla extract

1 cup chopped walnuts

1 cup no-sugar-added chocolate chips

The Cowboy Cookie is a chocolate chip cookie that has been beefed up with oats, coconut, nuts, and cinnamon. If you like texture, chewy goodness, and chocolate, Cowboy Cookies were made for you. Walnuts are high in omega-3 fatty acids, making them a wonderful addition to desserts, but you can substitute pecans or pistachios here as well. Shredded coconut is a great addition, adding an amazing chewy texture while bolstering the natural sweetness of the cookie.

1. Preheat the oven to 350°F. Line a baking sheet with parchment paper.

2. In a large bowl, combine the flour, shredded coconut, oats, sweetener, baking powder, cinnamon, and salt.

3. In a smaller bowl, whisk together the oil, eggs, and vanilla. Mix with the dry ingredients.

4. Stir in the walnuts and chocolate chips.

5. Scoop tablespoon-size cookies about 2 inches apart onto the prepared baking sheet.

6. Transfer the baking sheet to the oven and bake for 10 minutes, or until the cookies have lightly browned. Remove from the oven. Let cool on the sheet for 10 minutes, then transfer to a wire rack.

Make it last: Store the cookies in an airtight container for 5 days.

PER SERVING (2 COOKIES): *Calories: 220; Total fat: 20g; Total carbohydrates: 11g; Fiber: 6g; Net carbs: 5g; Added sugar: 0g; Protein: 5g*

Chocolate Chip Cookies

MAKES 24 COOKIES

PREP TIME: 10 minutes

COOK TIME: 10 minutes

1 cup whole-wheat flour

¼ cup coconut flour

1 teaspoon
  baking powder

¼ teaspoon salt

½ cup granulated
  sweetener of choice

2 large eggs

¼ cup avocado oil

¼ cup applesauce

1 teaspoon vanilla extract

½ cup no-sugar-added
  chocolate chips

Chocolate chip cookies are a classic, and this recipe delivers all the chocolaty goodness in a healthier whole-grain package. Using applesauce cuts the fat and gives the cookies a little added natural sweetness. The whole-wheat flour adds more fiber than all-purpose flour, and the avocado oil is an excellent way to add monounsaturated heart-healthy fat.

1. Preheat the oven to 350°F. Line a baking sheet with parchment paper.

2. In a medium bowl, combine the whole-wheat flour, coconut flour, baking powder, and salt.

3. In a large bowl, combine the sweetener, eggs, oil, applesauce, and vanilla. Mix in the dry ingredients until well blended.

4. Fold in the chocolate chips.

5. Scoop tablespoon-size balls about 2 inches apart onto the baking sheet. Using the palm of your hand, gently press the balls to flatten into cookies.

6. Transfer the baking sheet to the oven and bake for 10 to 12 minutes, or until the cookies have lightly browned. Remove from the oven. Let cool for 5 minutes on the sheet, then transfer to a wire rack to cool.

Make it last: Store the cookies in an airtight container for up to 1 week.

PER SERVING (2 COOKIES): *Calories: 130; Total fat: 8g; Total carbohydrates: 13g; Fiber: 4g; Net carbs: 9g; Added sugar: 0g; Protein: 3g*

Peanut Butter Cookies with Chocolate Chips

MAKES 16 COOKIES

PREP TIME: 10 minutes

COOK TIME: 10 minutes

¼ cup natural peanut butter

1 large egg

1 tablespoon coconut oil, melted

1 teaspoon vanilla extract

1 cup almond flour

¼ cup granulated sweetener of choice

1 teaspoon baking powder

Pinch salt

¼ cup no-sugar-added chocolate chips

Peanut butter and chocolate are a perfect pairing. These cookies are light, airy, and bursting with flavor. The peanut butter creates a wonderful texture in these gluten-free cookies, and by making a couple of easy swaps, they are low in carbs but bursting with warm and chocolaty goodness.

1. Preheat the oven to 325°F. Line a baking sheet with parchment paper.

2. In a large bowl, combine the peanut butter, egg, oil, and vanilla. Mix well.

3. Add the flour, sweetener, baking powder, and salt. Mix well.

4. Stir in the chocolate chips.

5. Scoop tablespoon-size cookies 1 inch apart onto the prepared baking sheet.

6. Transfer the baking sheet to the oven and bake for 8 to 10 minutes, or until the cookies are just golden brown. Remove from the oven. Let cool completely on the sheet.

Make it last: Store the cookies in an airtight container for up to 5 days.

PER SERVING (2 COOKIES): *Calories: 160; Total fat: 10g; Total carbohydrates: 6g; Fiber: 2g; Net carbs: 4g; Added sugar: 0g; Protein: 5g*

Frosted Pumpkin Cookies

MAKES 36 COOKIES

PREP TIME: 15 minutes

COOK TIME: 10 minutes

Pumpkin tends to be reserved for the fall, but these cookies are great any time of year. Just be sure to use plain pureed pumpkin and not pumpkin pie filling.

FOR THE COOKIES

1 cup whole-wheat flour

½ cup coconut flour

1 teaspoon baking soda

1 teaspoon ground cinnamon

½ teaspoon salt

½ cup avocado oil

¼ cup granulated sweetener of choice

1 cup canned pumpkin puree

2 large eggs

1 teaspoon vanilla extract

FOR THE FROSTING

4 ounces low-fat cream cheese, at room temperature

¼ cup granulated sweetener of choice

1 teaspoon vanilla extract

TO MAKE THE COOKIES

1. Preheat the oven to 350°F. Line a baking sheet with parchment paper.

2. In a large bowl, combine the whole-wheat flour, coconut flour, baking soda, cinnamon, and salt. Mix well.

3. In another large bowl, mix together the oil and sweetener. Stir in the pumpkin puree until mixed well. Add the eggs and vanilla. Stir to combine.

4. Add the flour mixture and mix well.

5. Scoop tablespoon-size balls onto the prepared baking sheet. Using the palm of your hand, gently press the balls to flatten into cookies.

6. Transfer the baking sheet to the oven, and bake for 8 to 10 minutes, or until the cookies have lightly browned. Remove from the oven. Transfer to a wire rack and let cool completely.

TO MAKE THE FROSTING

7. In a small bowl using a whisk or an electric mixer on high speed, whisk together the cream cheese, sweetener, and vanilla. Mix well.

8. Spread the frosting onto the cooled cookies.

PER SERVING (2 COOKIES): *Calories: 120; Total fat: 8g; Total carbohydrates: 8g; Fiber: 2g; Net carbs: 6g; Added sugar: 0g; Protein: 3g*

Chocolate-Dipped Biscotti

MAKES 16 BISCOTTI

PREP TIME: 15 minutes, plus 30 minutes for the dough to cool

COOK TIME: 45 minutes

1½ cups almond flour

½ cup sliced almonds

¼ cup granulated sweetener of choice

1 teaspoon baking powder

2 large eggs

3 tablespoons coconut oil, divided

¼ cup no-sugar-added chocolate chips

These take a little more time than the other cookie recipes because you must bake them twice to achieve the firm crispness of biscotti. But don't rush it. Be sure to let the biscotti cool before cutting them and allow for the slow final cooling to prevent crumbling. The biscotti are rather fragile until they are crisped, so handle with care at all stages of the process. To dress up this cookie, dip one side in melted chocolate for a gourmet flair. Try topping the chocolate side with some sprinkled nuts or toasted coconut for a little something extra.

1. Preheat the oven to 350°F. Line a baking sheet with parchment paper.

2. In a large bowl, combine the flour, almonds, sweetener, and baking powder. Mix well.

3. In another bowl, combine the eggs and 2 tablespoons of oil. Mix well.

4. Stir the wet ingredients into the dry ingredients and mix well to form a dough.

5. Turn out the dough onto the prepared baking sheet. Wet your hands to prevent sticking and use them to form the dough into a rectangle about 4 inches wide, 6 inches long, and 1 inch high.

6. Transfer the baking sheet to the oven and bake for 20 minutes, or until the dough has lightly browned. Remove from the oven. Let cool to room temperature, about 30 minutes.

7. Set the oven temperature to 300°F.

8. Using a sharp knife and a firm straight-down motion to prevent crumbling, cut the biscotti into slices about ½ inch thick.

9. Carefully arrange the slices on their sides in a single layer on the baking sheet.

10. Return the baking sheet to the oven. Bake for 10 to 15 minutes, carefully flip the biscotti, and bake for 10 more minutes, or until golden. Turn off the oven and crack open the oven door. Let the biscotti sit in the oven until completely cool and crisp.

11. When the biscotti are cool, in a small microwave-safe bowl, combine the chocolate chips and remaining 1 tablespoon of oil. Microwave on high for 30 seconds. Stir to combine. If needed, heat in 10-second intervals until melted.

12. Dip one end of a biscotto in the chocolate to coat, and transfer to a baking sheet. Repeat with the remaining biscotti, then transfer the sheet to the refrigerator for 30 minutes to set.

Make it last: Store the biscotti in an airtight container for up to 5 days.

PER SERVING: *Calories: 110; Total fat: 10g; Total carbohydrates: 4g; Fiber: 2g; Net carbs: 2g; Added sugar: 0g; Protein: 3g*

DOUBLE CHOCOLATE BROWNIES, PAGE 68

Chapter 4

Brownies and Bars

Apple Pie Bars

MAKES 12 BARS

PREP TIME: 35 minutes

COOK TIME: 15 minutes

¼ cup sliced almonds

¼ cup unsweetened shredded coconut

1½ cups almond flour

¼ cup pure maple syrup

¼ teaspoon salt

2 tablespoons coconut oil

3 medium apples, cored and thinly sliced

2 tablespoons granulated sweetener of choice

1 teaspoon apple pie spice

1 teaspoon vanilla extract

1 tablespoon water

1 recipe Vanilla Glaze (page 119)

You just can't beat the smell and taste of a freshly baked apple pie with a flaky crust and sweet cinnamon-y apples inside. These bars offer a lighter take on apple pie, using a mix of almond flour, chopped almonds, and coconut for added texture. Use a mix of sweet apples to create this recipe, such as Jonagold, Honeycrisp, Braeburn, Pink Lady. I like the natural sweetness, but use your favorite or mix up sweet and tart. Feel free to top these bars with Whipped Coconut Cream (page 121) or some reduced-sugar ice cream.

1. Preheat the oven to 350°F. Line an 8-inch square baking dish with parchment paper.

2. To make the crust, put the almonds and shredded coconut in a food processor. Pulse 2 or 3 times, or until coarsely chopped.

3. Mix in the flour, maple syrup, and salt.

4. Add the oil and mix until crumbly.

5. Press about three-quarters of the mixture into the prepared baking dish (reserving the rest).

6. Transfer the baking dish to the oven and bake for 10 minutes, or until the crust has lightly browned. Remove from the oven, leaving the oven on.

7. While the crust is baking, in a medium saucepan, combine the apples, sweetener, apple pie spice, and vanilla.

8. Add the water and bring to a simmer over medium heat.

9. Reduce the heat to low. Cook for 4 to 6 minutes, or until the apples have softened. Remove from the heat.

10. Spread the apple mixture over the pre-baked crust.

11. Sprinkle the remaining crust mixture over the top, pressing it into the apples.

12. Return the baking dish to the oven and bake for 20 to 25 minutes, or until the top is golden brown. Remove from the oven. Let cool completely.

13. Drizzle with the glaze. Cut into 12 bars.

Make it last: Store the bars in an airtight container in the refrigerator for up to 5 days.

PER SERVING (1 BAR): *Calories: 160; Total fat: 11g; Total carbohydrates: 14g; Fiber: 3g; Net carbs: 11g; Added sugar: 5g; Protein: 3g*

Blueberry
Crumble Bars

MAKES 12 BARS

PREP TIME: 15 minutes

COOK TIME: 45 minutes

1½ cups almond flour, plus
   1 tablespoon

¾ cup granulated
   sweetener of
   choice, divided

¼ cup coconut flour

1 teaspoon
   baking powder

¼ teaspoon salt

½ cup avocado oil

1 large egg

2 cups frozen or fresh
   blueberries

Grated zest and juice
   of 1 lemon

Blueberries are loaded with fiber and antioxidants, making them a perfect addition to any dessert–but any other berries, such as strawberries, blackberries, or raspberries, can work here, too. However, if you do use other berries, decrease the sweetener to just the ½ cup in the crumble.

1. Preheat the oven to 350°F. Line an 8-inch square baking dish with parchment paper.

2. To make the dough, in a large bowl, combine 1½ cups of almond flour, ½ cup of sweetener, the coconut flour, baking powder, and salt.

3. Add the oil and egg. Mix until the dough is crumbly.

4. Press half of the dough into the bottom of the prepared baking dish (reserve the other half).

5. In a small pot, combine the blueberries, remaining ¼ cup of sweetener, the lemon zest and juice, and remaining 1 tablespoon of flour. Simmer for 2 to 3 minutes over medium heat, pressing the berries using a potato masher or a fork until broken down and soft. Remove from the heat. Spread over the crust in the dish.

6. Crumble the remaining dough mixture over the berries.

7. Transfer the baking dish to the oven and bake for 35 to 40 minutes, or until the top has browned. Remove from the oven. Let cool completely, then cut into 12 bars.

Make it last: Store the bars in an airtight container in the refrigerator for up to 5 days.

PER SERVING (1 BAR): *Calories: 200; Total fat: 16g; Total carbohydrates: 7g; Fiber: 3g; Net carbs: 4g; Added sugar: 2g; Protein: 4g*

Raspberry Oatmeal Bars

MAKES 16 BARS

PREP TIME: 15 minutes

COOK TIME: 25 minutes

1½ cups
old-fashioned oats

1 large banana, peeled
and mashed

2 tablespoons granulated
sweetener of choice,
plus ¼ cup

3 tablespoons coconut oil,
melted, divided

1 teaspoon vanilla
extract, divided

1½ cups fresh or frozen
raspberries

½ cup almond flour

1 tablespoon coconut flour

1 recipe Vanilla Glaze
(page 119)

The banana is a wonderful complement to the
raspberries in these simple, hearty bars. Mixed with
old-fashioned oats, these gluten-free bars are bursting with flavor and sturdy enough to transport for
a sweet treat at work or to enjoy on the go. To add
sweetness, use more ripe bananas, or you can add a
spoonful of sweetener, honey, or pure maple syrup.

1. Preheat the oven to 350°F. Line an 8-inch square
    baking dish with parchment paper, with some
    paper overhanging the sides.

2. In a medium bowl, combine the oats, banana,
    2 tablespoons of sweetener, 1 tablespoon of oil,
    and ½ teaspoon of vanilla.

3. Press the mixture into the bottom of the prepared baking dish.

4. In a small bowl, lightly break the raspberries into
    pieces, but don't mash completely. Evenly spread
    on top of the oat mixture.

5. To make the topping, in a medium bowl, combine the almond flour, coconut flour, remaining
    ¼ cup of sweetener, 2 tablespoons of oil, and
    ½ teaspoon of vanilla. Mix well until the texture
    resembles wet sand.

6. Crumble the topping evenly over the raspberry layer and press it in.

7. Transfer the baking dish to the oven and bake for 20 to 25 minutes, or until the bars are lightly browned and firm. Remove from the oven. Let cool in the baking dish for 5 minutes.

8. Drizzle with the glaze, then lift the parchment paper out and remove the bars. Let cool to room temperature. Cut into 16 pieces.

Make it last: Store the bars in an airtight container in the refrigerator for up to 1 week.

PER SERVING (1 BAR): *Calories: 90; Total fat: 5g; Total carbohydrates: 9g; Fiber: 2g; Net carbs: 7g; Added sugar: 0g; Protein: 2g*

Lighter Lemon Bars

MAKES 12 BARS

PREP TIME: 15 minutes, plus 2 hours to chill

COOK TIME: 40 minutes

¼ cup avocado oil

2 tablespoons granulated sweetener of choice, plus ½ cup

1 cup almond flour

½ cup coconut flour

Pinch salt

4 large eggs

¾ cup freshly squeezed lemon juice

2 teaspoons minced lemon zest

Powdered sweetener of choice, for dusting

This recipe has all the contrast of sweet and sour for the perfect lemon bar without the sugar rush. For best results, make sure to use freshly squeezed lemon juice rather than bottled and do not forget the lemon zest. Use about one small lemon to yield 2 teaspoons of lemon zest and about six lemons for the juice.

1. Preheat the oven to 350°F. Line an 8-inch square baking dish with parchment paper.

2. In a large bowl, mix together the oil and 2 tablespoons of granulated sweetener.

3. Add the almond flour, coconut flour, and salt. Mix to form a dough.

4. Press the dough into the prepared baking dish.

5. Transfer the baking dish to the oven, and bake for 10 to 12 minutes, or until the dough has lightly browned. Remove from the oven.

6. Reduce the oven temperature to 325°F.

7. In a medium bowl, whisk the eggs well.

8. Whisk in the lemon juice and zest and remaining ½ cup of granulated sweetener. Pour over the dough.

9. Return the baking dish to the oven and bake for 20 to 25 minutes, or until the filling is lightly golden and set in the center. Remove from the oven. Let cool to room temperature, then refrigerate for at least 2 hours. Cut into 12 bars.

10. Dust the bars with powdered sweetener.

PER SERVING (1 BAR): *Calories: 140; Total fat: 11g; Total carbohydrates: 5g; Fiber: 3g; Net carbs: 2g; Added sugar: 2g; Protein: 5g*

Almond Butter Snickerdoodle Bars

MAKES 12 BARS

PREP TIME: 15 minutes

COOK TIME: 25 minutes

Avocado oil, for greasing

2½ cups almond flour

1½ teaspoons
  baking powder

1 teaspoon ground
  cinnamon, divided

2 large eggs

½ cup brown sweetener
  of choice

½ cup almond butter

1 teaspoon vanilla extract

2 tablespoons granulated
  sweetener of choice

Almond butter has all the creamy texture of peanut butter with a subtler nutty flavor for these cinnamon-sweet bars. Granulated white and brown sweetener is used to give the snickerdoodles that classic molasses flavor. If you prefer, use maple syrup instead of the brown sweetener for a more natural alternative. Just make sure to adjust for the added carbs!

1. Preheat the oven to 325°F. Grease an 8-inch square baking dish with avocado oil.

2. In a medium bowl, combine the flour, baking powder, and ½ teaspoon of cinnamon. Mix to combine.

3. In a large bowl, combine the eggs, brown sweetener, almond butter, and vanilla. Mix well.

4. To make the dough, stir in the dry ingredients and mix until just combined. Transfer to the prepared baking dish. Using a spatula, flatten the surface.

5. In a small bowl, combine the granulated sweetener and remaining ½ teaspoon of cinnamon. Mix well. Sprinkle on top of the dough.

6. Transfer the baking dish to the oven and bake for 20 to 25 minutes, or until the dough has lightly browned. Remove from the oven. Let cool completely, then cut into 12 bars.

Make it last: Store the bars in an airtight container in the refrigerator for up to 4 days.

PER SERVING (1 BAR): *Calories: 200; Total fat: 17g; Total carbohydrates: 6g; Fiber: 3g; Net carbs: 3g; Added sugar: 0g; Protein: 7g*

Sugar Cookie Bars

MAKES 12 BARS

PREP TIME: 10 minutes

COOK TIME: 35 minutes

2¼ cups almond flour

½ cup granulated
   sweetener of choice

¼ cup coconut flour

½ teaspoon baking soda

¼ cup plus 2 tablespoons
   avocado oil

1 large egg

1 tablespoon
   vanilla extract

1 recipe Cream Cheese
   Frosting (page 122)

The dough for these sugar cookie bars is a little thicker than for a cookie, making them fluffy and soft. They're topped with a cream cheese frosting; you can add a few drops of natural food coloring or mix in erythritol-based sugar-free sprinkles for a pop of color.

1. Preheat the oven to 350°F. Line an 8-inch square baking dish with parchment paper, with some paper overhanging the sides.

2. In a large bowl, combine the almond flour, sweetener, coconut flour, and baking soda.

3. Add the oil, egg, and vanilla. Mix to combine until a wet dough forms.

4. Press the dough into the prepared baking dish. Cover with aluminum foil.

5. Transfer the baking dish to the oven and bake for 20 minutes. Uncover and bake for 15 more minutes, or until the dough is lightly browned and firm. Remove from the oven. Let cool for 15 minutes, then use the parchment paper to remove the bars from the baking dish. Let cool completely.

6. Spread with the frosting. Cut into 12 pieces.

Make it last: Store the bars in an airtight container in the refrigerator for up to 5 days.

PER SERVING: *Calories: 210; Total fat: 17g; Total carbohydrates: 10g; Fiber: 3g; Net carbs: 7g; Added sugar: 0g; Protein: 6g*

Chocolate Chip Cookie Cheesecake Bars

MAKES 12 BARS

PREP TIME: 15 minutes, plus 4 hours to chill

COOK TIME: 40 minutes

If you love chocolate chip cookies and cheesecake, you are going to love this merger! The base is a chocolate chip cookie, then there's a cheesecake filling, then a cookie crumble top. Brown sweetener, such as erythritol, lends a delicious flavor to the cookie, but if you don't have it, you can use ½ cup of granulated sweetener plus 2 tablespoons of molasses instead.

FOR THE COOKIE BARS

⅓ cup avocado oil, plus more for greasing

2 cups almond flour

½ cup brown sweetener of choice

1 teaspoon baking powder

¼ teaspoon salt

1 large egg

1 teaspoon vanilla extract

½ cup no-sugar-added chocolate chips

FOR THE CHEESECAKE LAYER

1 (8-ounce) package low-fat cream cheese, at room temperature

¼ cup powdered sweetener of choice

1 large egg

2 tablespoons milk of choice

1 teaspoon vanilla extract

TO MAKE THE COOKIE BARS

1. Preheat the oven to 325°F. Grease an 8-inch square baking dish with avocado oil.

2. In a medium bowl, combine the flour, brown sweetener, baking powder, and salt.

3. Add the oil, egg, and vanilla. Mix until the dough comes together.

4. Fold in the chocolate chips.

5. Press three-quarters of the dough into the prepared baking dish, reserving the rest for the topping.

6. Transfer the baking dish to the oven and bake for 12 to 15 minutes, or until the edges have browned. Remove from the oven, leaving the oven on. Let the dough cool completely.

TO MAKE THE CHEESECAKE LAYER

7. In a large bowl using a handheld electric mixer, beat the cream cheese on medium-high speed for 1 to 2 minutes, or until smooth.

8. Add the powdered sweetener and beat until well combined.

9. Add the egg, milk, and vanilla. Beat until smooth. Turn off the mixer.

10. Spread the mixture over the top of the cooled cookie dough.

11. Crumble the reserved raw dough over the mixture and press it lightly into the surface.

12. Return the baking dish to the oven and bake for 20 to 25 minutes, or until the dough is golden brown. Remove from the oven. Let cool to room temperature, then refrigerate for 4 hours, or until chilled and set. Cut into 12 bars.

Make it last: Store the bars in an airtight container in the refrigerator for up to 5 days.

PER SERVING (1 BAR): *Calories: 230; Total fat: 20g; Total carbohydrates: 8g; Fiber: 4g; Net carbs: 4g; Added sugar: 0g; Protein: 6g*

No-Bake Dark Chocolate Cheesecake Bars

MAKES 8 BARS

PREP TIME: 10 minutes, plus 2 hours to chill

1 cup almond flour

8 tablespoons granulated sweetener of choice, divided

¼ cup unsweetened cocoa powder

1 teaspoon vanilla extract

1 to 2 tablespoons milk of choice

⅓ cup no-sugar-added dark chocolate chips

4 ounces low-fat cream cheese, at room temperature

The only thing that can make rich cheesecake better is chocolate! These no-bake bars boast both dark chocolate and cocoa powder for a truly decadent work of culinary art. And for a final flourish, they're topped with sweetened cream cheese.

1. Line an 8-by-4-inch loaf pan with parchment paper.

2. To make the dough, in a bowl, combine the flour, 6 tablespoons of sweetener, the cocoa powder, and vanilla. Mix well.

3. Add the milk, mixing after each tablespoon, until the dough comes together but is not wet.

4. Stir in the chocolate chips.

5. Transfer the dough to the prepared pan and press in evenly.

6. In a small bowl, mix together the cream cheese and remaining 2 tablespoons of sweetener until mixed well.

7. Spread the cream cheese mixture over the top of the dough. Refrigerate for at least 2 hours. Cut into 8 bars.

Make it last: Store the bars in an airtight container in the refrigerator for up to 1 week, or freeze for up to 2 months.

PER SERVING (1 BAR): *Calories: 100; Total fat: 7g, Total carbohydrates: 9g, Fiber: 4g, Net carbs: 5g, Added sugar: 1g, Protein 3g*

Perfect Blondies

MAKES 12 BLONDIES

PREP TIME: 10 minutes

COOK TIME: 25 minutes

¼ cup coconut oil, at room temperature, plus more for greasing

1 (15-ounce) can chickpeas, drained

1 cup almond flour

½ cup pure maple syrup

2 large eggs

1 teaspoon baking soda

1 teaspoon vanilla extract

¼ teaspoon salt

½ cup no-sugar-added chocolate chips

Chickpeas are not the first thing you might think of for a dessert recipe, but they lend a buttery flavor to this easy blondie recipe—not to mention wonderful plant-based protein and fiber. Like other recipes made in a food processor, these are really quick to put together. Just be sure to make a smooth batter by blending the chickpeas for a minute or two so that they are undetectable in the finished blondie. To reduce carbs, use ¼ to ½ cup of natural granulated sweetener of your choice in place of the maple syrup.

1. Preheat the oven to 350°F. Grease an 8-inch square baking dish with coconut oil.

2. To make the batter, in a food processor, combine the chickpeas, almond flour, maple syrup, oil, eggs, baking soda, vanilla, and salt. Process well until smooth.

3. Fold in the chocolate chips.

4. Pour the batter into the prepared baking dish.

5. Transfer the baking dish to the oven and bake for 20 to 25 minutes, or until the batter is set. Remove from the oven. Let cool completely, then cut into 12 pieces.

Make it last: Store the blondies for up to 5 days in an airtight container in the refrigerator.

PER SERVING (1 BLONDIE): *Calories: 190; Total fat: 12g; Total carbohydrates: 19g; Fiber: 5g; Net carbs: 14g; Added sugar: 9g; Protein: 5g*

Double Chocolate Brownies

MAKES 9 BROWNIES

PREP TIME: 10 minutes

COOK TIME: 30 minutes

2 tablespoons avocado oil, plus more for greasing

1 (15-ounce) can black beans, drained and rinsed

½ cup granulated sweetener of choice

¼ cup unsweetened cocoa powder

¼ cup unsweetened applesauce

¼ cup oat flour

2 large eggs

2 teaspoons vanilla extract

1 teaspoon baking powder

¼ teaspoon salt

½ cup no sugar added chocolate chips

½ cup chopped walnuts

Using blended beans in these chocolate brownies is a fantastic way to add phenomenal texture while punching up the protein and fiber for improved blood sugar control. The extra chocolate chips add more chocolaty richness and, combined with the walnuts, give a nice texture contrast, so be sure not to skip them.

1. Preheat the oven to 350°F. Grease an 8-inch square baking dish with avocado oil.

2. Put the beans, sweetener, cocoa powder, applesauce, oat flour, eggs, oil, vanilla, baking powder, and salt in a food processor or blender. Process until smooth.

3. Stir in the chocolate chips.

4. Pour the mixture into the prepared baking dish.

5. Sprinkle the walnuts on top.

6. Transfer the baking dish to the oven and bake for 25 to 30 minutes, or until the batter is set. Remove from the oven. Let cool completely, then cut into 12 pieces.

Make it last: Store the brownies in an airtight container in the refrigerator for up to 5 days.

PER SERVING: *Calories: 186; Total fat: 11g, Total carbohydrates: 14g; Fiber: 3g, Net carbs: 11g; Added sugar: 1g; Protein: 6g*

Fudgy Chocolate-Mint Bars

MAKES 8 PIECES

PREP TIME: 10 minutes, plus 3 hours to chill

1 cup no-sugar-added chocolate chips, divided

¼ cup milk of choice

1 teaspoon vanilla extract

4 ounces low-fat cream cheese, at room temperature

¼ cup powdered sweetener of choice

1 teaspoon mint extract

These mint bars bring back wonderful memories of my college days, when my roommates and I would enjoy a batch for weekend movie nights. The touch of mint in the cream cheese layer on top of the fudgy layer will satisfy every chocolate craving. For extra elegance and crunch, top the brownies with no-sugar-added chocolate chips or cacao nibs. You can also turn these into an ice cream dessert by chilling them for a couple of hours in the freezer.

1. Line a 4-inch square baking dish with parchment paper, with some paper overhanging the sides.

2. Put ¾ cup of chocolate chips and the milk in a microwave-safe bowl. Microwave on high for 30-second intervals, stirring in between each interval, until melted.

3. Stir in the vanilla.

4. Pour the melted chocolate into the prepared baking dish. Refrigerate for 2 hours, or until set.

5. Put the cream cheese, sweetener, and mint extract in a medium bowl. Whisk to combine.

6. Stir in the remaining ¼ cup of chocolate chips.

7. Spread the mixture over the chocolate in the baking dish. Refrigerate for at least 1 hour to set. Then lift out of the dish and cut into 8 pieces.

Make it last: Store the bars in an airtight container for up to 2 weeks in the refrigerator.

PER SERVING (1 BROWNIE): *Calories: 110; Total fat: 8g; Total carbohydrates: 12g; Fiber: 6g; Net carbs: 6g; Added sugar: 0g; Protein: 3g*

CLASSIC CHEESECAKE, PAGE 88

Chapter 5
Cakes and Quick Breads

Two-Minute Chocolate Mug Cake

SERVES 1

PREP TIME: 5 minutes

COOK TIME: 2 minutes

2 teaspoons avocado oil, plus more for greasing

3 tablespoons almond flour

2 tablespoons unsweetened cocoa powder

2 tablespoons granulated sweetener of choice

1 large egg

1 teaspoon vanilla extract

¼ teaspoon baking powder

Pinch salt

Pinch unsweetened coconut flakes (optional)

When you need a treat, you're short on time, and you don't want any cleanup, a quick microwave mug cake is the perfect no-fuss dessert. This single-portion cake delivers a rich, chocolaty crumb that is great on its own or topped with Whipped Coconut Cream (page 121) or Cream Cheese Frosting (page 122). If you prefer, use 2 teaspoons of maple syrup in place of the granulated sweetener for a total of 15 grams net carbs (21 grams total carbs and 6 grams of fiber).

1. Grease an 8-ounce mug with avocado oil.

2. To make the batter, in a small bowl, combine the flour, cocoa powder, sweetener, egg, oil, vanilla, baking powder, and salt. Mix well. Pour the batter into the mug.

3. Sprinkle the coconut flakes (if using) over the top, and microwave on high for 1 minute to 1 minute 30 seconds, or until the cake is set. The time will vary based on the power of your microwave. Let cool for a few minutes, then enjoy.

Make it last: These are best served warm right from the microwave. However, you can mix all the dry ingredients in individual portions to have on hand to quickly make a single-serving cake on the go. When you're ready to bake, add an egg and the oil, mix, and pour into a mug to microwave.

PER SERVING (1 MUG WITHOUT COCONUT FLAKES): *Calories: 310; Total fat: 24g; Total carbohydrates: 8g; Fiber: 4g; Net carbs: 4g; Added sugar: 1g; Protein: 12g*

Mini Cherry No-Bake Cheesecake Bites

MAKES 12 BITES

PREP TIME: 15 minutes, plus 1 hour to chill

COOK TIME: 1 minute

1 cup almond flour

3 tablespoons coconut oil, melted

1 (8-ounce) package low-fat cream cheese, at room temperature

¼ cup plain low-fat Greek yogurt

2 tablespoons honey

1 teaspoon vanilla extract

½ cup chopped dark, sweet frozen cherries, plus more for garnish

These mini cheesecake bites are perfect for when you don't want to bother with cooking but still want that rich cheesecake texture and flavor. Individually portioned in a muffin tin, these are perfect for storing in the freezer and pulling out when you want a sweet treat.

1. In a small bowl, combine the flour and oil. Mix well. Press 1 heaping tablespoon of the mixture into each cup of a 12-cup muffin tin.

2. In a medium bowl using a handheld electric mixer, combine the cream cheese, yogurt, honey, and vanilla on medium speed. Mix well. Turn off the mixer.

3. Divide the mixture among the muffin cups.

4. In a small microwave-safe dish, microwave the cherries on high for 20 to 30 seconds, or until warm. Stir and continue to heat in 20- to 30-second intervals until soft. Spoon over the cheesecakes, and freeze in the muffin tin for at least 1 hour. Pop the cheesecakes out of the tin, thaw, and serve.

Make it last: Store the bites in an airtight container for up to 5 days in the refrigerator, or freeze for up to 2 months.

PER SERVING (1 BITE): *Calories: 130; Total fat: 10g; Total carbohydrates: 7g; Fiber: 1g; Net carbs: 6g; Added sugar: 3g; Protein: 4g*

Low-Carb Banana Bread

MAKES 8 SLICES

PREP TIME: 10 minutes

COOK TIME: 35 minutes

2 tablespoons coconut oil, plus more for greasing, melted

1¼ cups almond flour

3 tablespoons granulated sweetener of choice

2 tablespoons coconut flour

2 teaspoons ground cinnamon

1 teaspoon baking powder

1 large ripe banana, peeled and mashed

3 large eggs

¼ cup chopped walnuts

In this version of gluten-free banana bread, almond flour and coconut flour form the base and walnuts add a little crunch. With just one banana, this version is lower in natural sugars than the classic, but I like to sweeten it with a natural sweetener to achieve the same taste. The trick is to use a very ripe banana for the best flavor: one that is soft to the touch, has a thin peel, and has black speckles and spots on the surface.

1. Preheat the oven to 350°F. Grease an 8-by-4-inch loaf pan with coconut oil.

2. In a small bowl, combine the almond flour, sweetener, coconut flour, cinnamon, and baking powder.

3. In a large bowl, combine the banana, eggs, and oil. Mix well.

4. Mix the dry ingredients into the wet ingredients. Transfer to the prepared pan.

5. Sprinkle the walnuts evenly over the top.

6. Transfer the pan to the oven and bake for 30 to 35 minutes, or until the top has browned and a knife inserted into the center comes out clean. Remove from the oven. Let cool completely before slicing.

Make it last: Store leftover banana bread in an airtight container in the refrigerator for up to 5 days.

PER SERVING (1 SLICE): *Calories: 190; Total fat: 16g; Total carbohydrates: 7g; Fiber: 3g; Net carbs: 4g; Added sugar: 2g; Protein: 6g*

Lemon-Blueberry Streusel Muffins

MAKES 12 MUFFINS

PREP TIME: 10 minutes

COOK TIME: 30 minutes

Blueberry and lemon are a perfect pair, and in this streusel-topped muffin, they perfectly highlight each other's complex flavors. Oat flour is available in many grocery stores these days, but if you can't find it or don't want an extra bag of flour sitting in your pantry, use an equal amount of old-fashioned oats and grind them in a blender or food processor until you have a fine powder.

FOR THE MUFFINS

Avocado oil, for greasing

1 cup oat flour

1 cup almond flour

½ cup granulated sweetener of choice

2 teaspoons baking powder

½ teaspoon salt

1 cup milk of choice

2 large eggs

1 tablespoon grated lemon zest

1 teaspoon vanilla extract

1 cup fresh or frozen blueberries

FOR THE TOPPING

2 tablespoons oat flour

2 tablespoons granulated sweetener of choice

1 teaspoon ground cinnamon

1 tablespoon avocado oil

TO MAKE THE MUFFINS

1. Preheat the oven to 375°F. Grease a 12-cup muffin tin with avocado oil.

2. To make the batter, in a large bowl, mix together the oat flour, almond flour, sweetener, baking powder, and salt.

3. Add the milk, eggs, lemon zest, and vanilla. Mix well.

4. Stir in the blueberries. Divide the batter among the cups of the prepared muffin tin.

TO MAKE THE TOPPING

5. In a small bowl, combine the oat flour, sweetener, and cinnamon.

6. Add the oil and mix well until the mixture resembles wet sand. Crumble the topping over the tops of the muffins.

7. Transfer the tin to the oven and bake for 25 to 30 minutes, or until the topping is golden brown. Remove from the oven.

PER SERVING (1 MUFFIN): *Calories: 110; Total fat: 7g; Total carbohydrates: 10g; Fiber: 2g; Net carbs: 8g; Added sugar: 0g; Protein: 4g*

Baked Cinnamon Sugar Donuts

MAKES 6 DONUTS

PREP TIME: 10 minutes

COOK TIME: 20 minutes

FOR THE DONUTS

¼ cup avocado oil, plus more for greasing

1 cup almond flour

¼ cup granulated sweetener of choice

1½ teaspoons baking powder

1 teaspoon ground cinnamon

Pinch salt

2 large eggs

1 teaspoon vanilla extract

FOR THE TOPPING

⅓ cup granulated sweetener of choice

1½ teaspoons ground cinnamon

2 tablespoons avocado oil

There is something magical about the smell of freshly baked cinnamon sugar donuts for breakfast. A natural granulated sweetener sweetens the dough and is also mixed with cinnamon to dust the exterior of the donuts. If you have a donut pan, this is the perfect time to use it. If not, you can easily get the job done using a muffin tin and placing a piece of rolled-up aluminum foil in each muffin cup. Another option is to bake the donuts as muffins, then use a cylinder cookie cutter to remove the centers. You can then roll the centers in cinnamon sugar to make donut holes.

TO MAKE THE DONUTS

1. Preheat the oven to 350°F. Grease a 6-cup donut pan with avocado oil.

2. In a large bowl, combine the flour, sweetener, baking powder, cinnamon, and salt.

3. In a small bowl, whisk together the oil, eggs, and vanilla.

4. Mix the wet ingredients into the dry ingredients.

5. Divide the mixture among the cups of the prepared donut pan, filling them about three-quarters of the way.

6. Transfer the pan to the oven, and bake for 18 to 22 minutes, or until the donuts are golden brown. Remove from the oven. Let cool for at least 15 minutes, or until the donuts have firmed up.

Continued ⟶

7. Run a knife around the inner and outer ring of the donuts, and remove them from the pan.

TO MAKE THE TOPPING

8. In a small bowl, combine the sweetener and cinnamon.

9. Brush the donuts with the oil.

10. Press the donuts into the sweetener mixture to coat.

Make it last: Store the donuts in an airtight container in the refrigerator for up to 3 days.

PER SERVING (1 DONUT): *Calories: 260; Total fat: 24g; Total carbohydrates: 4g; Fiber: 2g; Net carbs: 2g; Added sugar: 0g; Protein: 5g*

Angel Food Cake

SERVES 8

PREP TIME: 15 minutes

COOK TIME: 45 minutes

½ cup almond flour

¼ cup coconut flour

6 large egg whites, at room temperature

2 teaspoons distilled white vinegar

½ cup granulated sweetener of choice

1 teaspoon vanilla extract

This Angel Food Cake has a tasty, fluffy sponge texture, and although it's divine on its own, you can up the gourmet factor by drizzling on Berry Fruit Sauce (page 118). This cake does not use any butter or oil, making it rather light and extremely satisfying.

1. Preheat the oven to 350°F.

2. In a small bowl, combine the almond flour and coconut flour.

3. In a large bowl using a handheld electric mixer, beat the egg whites and vinegar on high speed for 4 to 6 minutes, or until soft peaks form.

4. Add the sweetener and vanilla. Mix to combine. Turn off the mixer.

5. To make the batter, fold the dry ingredients into the egg whites until just combined. Transfer to an ungreased 8-inch tube pan or 8-by-4-inch loaf pan. Using a spatula, spread out the batter.

6. Transfer the pan to the oven and bake for 45 minutes, or until the top has lightly browned. Remove from the oven. Let cool for 15 minutes, or until the cake has firmed up slightly.

7. Invert the pan and let the cake cool completely.

8. Once cool, run a knife along the edges of the pan to release the cake.

Make it last: Store the cake in an airtight container at room temperature for up to 3 days.

PER SERVING: *Calories: 70; Total fat: 3.5g; Total carbohydrates: 4g; Fiber: 2g; Net carbs: 2g; Added sugar: 0g; Protein: 5g*

Carrot Cake with Cream Cheese Frosting

SERVES 12

PREP TIME: 15 minutes

COOK TIME: 25 minutes

Avocado oil, for greasing

1½ cups coconut flour

1 tablespoon ground
  cinnamon

2 teaspoons
  baking powder

½ teaspoon salt

½ teaspoon
  ground nutmeg

6 large eggs

½ cup plain low-fat
  Greek yogurt

⅓ cup sweetener of choice

1 teaspoon vanilla extract

2 cups grated carrots

1 cup walnut
  halves, divided

2 recipes Cream Cheese
  Frosting (page 122)

Carrot cake is loaded with beta-carotene-rich carrots and heart-healthy omega-3 fatty acid-rich walnuts, making it one of my favorite ways to indulge. To make it even better, this cake uses coconut flour and Greek yogurt, which gives a boost in protein while delivering a light-textured crumb. To tie it all together, it's topped with a thick layer of sweet Cream Cheese Frosting.

1. Preheat the oven to 350°F. Grease an 8-inch cake pan with avocado oil.

2. In a large bowl, mix together the coconut flour, cinnamon, baking powder, salt, and nutmeg.

3. In a medium bowl, whisk together the eggs, yogurt, sweetener, and vanilla.

4. Stir the carrots into the medium bowl and mix well.

5. To make the batter, fold the wet ingredients into the dry ingredients and mix until no dry bits remain.

6. Chop ¾ cup of walnut halves, and fold them into the batter. Transfer to the prepared cake pan.

7. Transfer the pan to the oven and bake for 20 to 25 minutes, or until the top has lightly browned. Remove from the oven. Let cool for 15 minutes.

8. Invert the pan to remove the cake and let cool completely at room temperature.

9. When the cake is cool, frost with the cream cheese frosting and top with the remaining ¼ cup of walnuts for decoration.

Make it last: Store the cake covered in the refrigerator for up to 4 days.

PER SERVING: *Calories: 190; Total fat: 11g; Total carbohydrates: 12g; Fiber: 6g; Net carbs: 6g; Added sugar: 0g; Protein: 8g*

Funfetti Birthday Cake

SERVES 16

PREP TIME: 15 minutes

COOK TIME: 25 minutes

½ cup coconut oil, plus more for greasing

2 cups almond flour, plus more for dusting

1 cup coconut flour

2 teaspoons baking powder

½ teaspoon salt

1 cup granulated sweetener of choice

6 egg whites (¾ cup), at room temperature

1 tablespoon vanilla extract

¾ cup milk of choice

⅓ cup sugar-free rainbow sprinkles

1 recipe Cream Cheese Frosting (page 122)

Maybe it's your birthday, or you just need some fun and sprinkles in your life. This gluten-free Funfetti cake is just the thing to make you feel like a kid again. Look for sugar-free sprinkles in a well-stocked baking section of a grocery store or natural food market, or order them online. Good Dee's and Stoka are two brands that make erythritol-sweetened sprinkles that work well for this cake.

1. Preheat the oven to 350°F. Grease 2 (8-inch) cake pans with coconut oil, then dust with almond flour.

2. In a small bowl, mix together the almond flour, coconut flour, baking powder, and salt.

3. In a large bowl using a handheld electric mixer, beat the oil and sweetener on medium speed.

4. Add the egg whites and vanilla. Beat until combined.

5. Add the milk and mix well, scraping down the sides as needed.

6. Add the dry ingredients and mix well. Turn off the mixer.

7. Fold in the sprinkles until evenly distributed.

8. Divide the mixture between the prepared pans. Using a spatula, smooth out the tops.

9. Transfer the pans to the oven and bake for 20 to 25 minutes, or until the cakes have browned lightly around the edges. Remove from the oven. Let cool for about 20 minutes.

10. Invert each cake onto a plate to remove from the pans. Transfer to a wire rack. Let cool completely.

11. Frost 1 cake with half of the cream cheese frosting. Stack the second cake on top, and frost it as well.

Make it last: Store the cake covered in the refrigerator for up to 5 days.

PER SERVING: *Calories: 190; Total fat: 15g; Total carbohydrates: 8g; Fiber: 4g; Net carbs: 4g; Added sugar: 2g; Protein: 5g*

Red Velvet Cupcakes

MAKES 10 CUPCAKES

PREP TIME: 15 minutes

COOK TIME: 20 minutes

¼ cup avocado oil, plus more for greasing

3 large eggs

1 tablespoon distilled white vinegar

2 teaspoons vanilla extract

10 to 20 drops red food coloring

1 cup almond flour

½ cup granulated sweetener of choice

1 tablespoon unsweetened cocoa powder

1 teaspoon baking powder

1 recipe Cream Cheese Frosting (page 122)

Light and moist, red velvet cupcakes are a delightful break from the ordinary. Just a touch of chocolate, topped with a sweet yet savory cream cheese frosting, creates a splendid contrast of flavors for your taste buds. Use a natural red food coloring to give them their distinctive red velvety color.

1. Preheat the oven to 350°F. Grease 10 cups of a 12-cup muffin tin with avocado oil.

2. In a large bowl, whisk together the eggs, oil, vinegar, vanilla, and food coloring.

3. In a small bowl, mix together the almond flour, sweetener, cocoa powder, and baking powder.

4. To make the batter, add the dry ingredients to the wet ingredients and stir until just mixed.

5. Divide the batter among the cups of the prepared muffin tin, filling them about two-thirds of the way.

6. Transfer the muffin tin to the oven and bake for 12 minutes. Turn the muffin tin around and bake for 10 minutes, or until the tops are golden brown. Remove from the oven. Let cool completely.

7. Frost the cupcakes with the cream cheese frosting.

Make it last: Store leftover cupcakes in an airtight container in the refrigerator for up 5 days.

PER SERVING (1 CUPCAKE): *Calories: 140; Total fat: 12g; Total carbohydrates: 4g; Fiber: 1g; Net carbs: 3g; Added sugar: 0g; Protein: 4g*

Triple Chocolate Cake

SERVES 10

PREP TIME: 15 minutes

COOK TIME: 30 minutes

2 tablespoons avocado oil, plus more for greasing

1½ cups almond flour

2 tablespoons coconut flour

½ cup unsweetened cocoa powder

2 teaspoons baking powder

½ teaspoon salt

½ cup milk of choice

½ cup granulated sweetener of choice

2 large eggs, at room temperature

1 teaspoon vanilla extract

1 recipe Cream Cheese Frosting (page 122)

¼ cup unsweetened cocoa powder

This cake is loaded with chocolate flavor and has a lovely moist texture. Using just ½ cup of granulated sweetener, it's a chocolaty cake that is lightly sweetened. The Cream Cheese Frosting mixed with a generous amount of cocoa powder pulls it all together for a double chocolate treat with the perfect level of sweetness. For a different flavor, try this with Almond Buttercream Frosting (page 123) instead. This recipe makes one 8-inch round cake, so if you wish to make a double layer cake, just double the recipe and make two.

1. Preheat the oven to 350°F. Grease an 8-inch cake pan with avocado oil.

2. In a large bowl, combine the almond flour, coconut flour, cocoa powder, baking powder, and salt. Mix well.

3. In a medium bowl, mix together the milk, sweetener, eggs, oil, and vanilla. Stir well.

4. Add the wet ingredients to the dry ingredients and mix well. Transfer to the prepared pan.

5. Transfer the pan to the oven and bake for 25 to 30 minutes, or until the cake is just set. Remove from the oven. Let cool for 15 minutes.

6. Run a knife around the pan to release the cake, and invert over a plate to remove from the pan. Transfer to a wire rack. Let cool completely.

7. To make the frosting, in a large bowl using an electric mixer, combine the cream cheese frosting and cocoa powder on medium-high speed. Mix well. Turn off the mixer.

8. When the cake is cool, frost it all over.

Make it last: Store the frosted cake covered in the refrigerator for up to 4 days.

PER SERVING: *Calories: 230; Total fat: 19g; Total carbohydrates: 7g; Fiber: 4g; Net carbs: 3g; Added sugar: 0g; Protein: 8g*

Classic Cheesecake

SERVES 16

PREP TIME: 15 minutes, plus 4 hours to chill

COOK TIME: 55 minutes

2 cups almond flour

2 tablespoons granulated sweetener of choice

⅓ cup avocado oil

2 teaspoons vanilla extract, divided

3 (8-ounce) packages low-fat cream cheese, at room temperature

1 cup powdered sweetener of choice

3 large eggs

⅓ cup blueberries

⅓ cup quartered strawberries

⅓ cup blackberries

1 tablespoon honey

This recipe is a take on the classic rich and delicious cheesecake but without the blood sugar spike. The powdered sweetener blends in perfectly to create a creamy and delicious filling. Although this cheesecake is beautiful and an absolute delight as is, feel free to add extra flavor (and antioxidants) by topping it with Berry Fruit Sauce (page 118) in place of the strawberries, blackberries, blueberries, and honey.

1. Preheat the oven to 350°F. Line a 9-inch pie pan with parchment paper, or grease a 9-inch springform pan with avocado oil.

2. To make the crust, in a medium bowl, mix together the flour and granulated sweetener.

3. Add the oil and 1 teaspoon of vanilla.

4. Press the crust into the bottom of the prepared pan.

5. Transfer the pan to the oven and bake for 10 minutes, or until the crust has just lightly browned. Remove from the oven, leaving the oven on. Let cool.

6. To make the filling, in a medium bowl using a handheld electric mixer, beat together the cream cheese, powdered sweetener, eggs, and remaining 1 teaspoon of vanilla on medium speed for 2 to 3 minutes, or until smooth. Turn off the mixer.

7. Pour the filling into the crust, and using a spatula, smooth the surface.

8. Return the pan to the oven and bake for 45 minutes, or until the center is just set. Remove from the oven. Let cool to room temperature, then refrigerate for 4 hours, or until chilled.

9. Sprinkle the strawberries, blackberries, and blueberries over the top and drizzle with the honey to serve.

Make it last: Store the cheesecake covered in the refrigerator for up to 5 days.

PER SERVING: *Calories: 212; Total fat: 19g; Total carbohydrates: 8g; Fiber: 2g; Net carbs: 6g; Added sugar: 0g; Protein: 5g*

Chocolate-Hazelnut Crunch Cheesecake

SERVES 16

PREP TIME: 15 minutes, plus 4 hours to chill

COOK TIME: 1 hour 25 minutes

Chocolate-hazelnut spread transforms this cheesecake into an out-of-body experience. Look for a naturally sweetened hazelnut spread in a well-stocked super-market, natural food store, or online. Sweetened with erythritol or stevia, these creamy hazelnut spreads keep the carbs low while giving the cake a creamy, chocolaty richness. For added crunch, be generous with the chopped hazelnuts on top.

FOR THE CRUST

1½ cups almond flour

3 tablespoons avocado oil

2 tablespoons granulated sweetener of choice

FOR THE CHEESECAKE

2 (8-ounce) packages low-fat cream cheese, at room temperature

¼ cup granulated sweetener of choice

2 large eggs

¼ cup milk of choice

2 tablespoons unsweetened cocoa powder, plus more for garnish

2 teaspoons vanilla extract

1 cup no-sugar-added chocolate-hazelnut spread

1 recipe Whipped Coconut Cream (page 121)

¼ cup chopped hazelnuts

TO MAKE THE CRUST

1. Preheat the oven to 350°F.

2. In a small bowl, mix together the flour, oil, and sweetener. Stir well. Transfer to a 9-inch springform pan.

3. Press the crust into the bottom of the pan.

4. Transfer the dish to the oven and bake for 10 minutes. Remove from the oven, leaving the oven on. Set aside to cool.

TO MAKE THE CHEESECAKE

5. In a large bowl using a handheld electric mixer, beat together the cream cheese and sweet-ener on medium speed for 2 to 3 minutes, or until smooth.

6. Add the eggs one at a time, mixing between each addition.

7. Add the milk, 2 tablespoons of cocoa powder, and vanilla. Mix well.

8. Add the hazelnut spread and mix until combined. Turn off the mixer.

9. Using a spatula, transfer the mixture to the baked crust.

10. Return the dish to the oven and bake for 1 hour to 1 hour 15 minutes, or until the cake is set in the center. Turn off the oven. Open the oven door a few inches and let the cake cool completely without moving it.

11. Transfer the cooled cheesecake to the refrigerator and chill for at least 4 hours.

12. Spread the whipped cream on top and sprinkle with cocoa powder. Top with the chopped hazelnuts to serve.

Make it last: Store the cheesecake covered in the refrigerator for up to 5 days.

PER SERVING: *Calories: 254; Total fat: 22g; Total carbohydrates: 15g; Fiber: 7g; Net carbs: 8g; Added sugar: 3g; Protein: 6g*

PUMPKIN PIE, PAGE 106

Chapter 6
Pies and Tarts

Blueberry and Strawberry Creamy Fruit Tart

SERVES 8

PREP TIME: 15 minutes, plus 2 hours to chill

COOK TIME: 15 minutes

2 cups almond flour

Pinch salt

2 tablespoons coconut oil, melted

1 large egg white

6 ounces silken tofu

1 cup plain low-fat Greek yogurt

¼ cup pure maple syrup or granulated sweetener of your choice

1 tablespoon freshly squeezed lemon juice

1 cup fresh blueberries

1 cup sliced fresh strawberries

In this quick fruit tart, tofu and yogurt create a fluffy filling that sets the stage for the berries, which add natural sweetness to the maple syrup-sweetened filling. The basic almond flour crust bakes nice and crisp while you prepare the filling, allowing this dessert to be prepared in just minutes, ready to be chilled.

1. Preheat the oven to 350°F.

2. To make the crust, in a medium bowl, mix together the almond flour and salt.

3. Drizzle with the oil and mix well.

4. Mix in the egg white and stir to combine. Transfer to a 9-inch pie dish.

5. Using your hands or the bottom of a measuring cup, press the crust into the bottom of the dish and up the sides. Prick all over with a fork.

6. Transfer the dish to the oven and bake for 15 minutes, or until the crust has lightly browned. Remove from the oven. Set aside to cool.

7. Put the tofu, yogurt, maple syrup, and lemon juice in a food processor or blender. Process until smooth.

8. Transfer the mixture to the cooled piecrust, and using a spatula, smooth the filling. Chill for 2 hours, or until set.

9. Arrange the blueberries and strawberries over the top of the filling before serving.

PER SERVING: *Calories: 250; Total fat: 17g; Total carbohydrates: 17g; Fiber: 4g; Net carbs: 13g; Added sugar: 7g; Protein: 10g*

Triple Berry
Crumble Cobbler

SERVES 6

PREP TIME: 10 minutes

COOK TIME: 25 minutes

1 cup fresh or frozen
   raspberries

1 cup fresh or frozen
   blueberries

1 cup fresh or frozen
   blackberries

4 tablespoons
   granulated sweetener
   blend, divided

¾ cup almond flour

3 tablespoons
   coconut flour

1 teaspoon grated
   lemon zest

1 large egg

2 tablespoons avocado oil

½ teaspoon vanilla extract

A crumble is an easy dessert to throw together in minutes and comes out great with little effort. Here the trio of raspberries, blueberries, and blackberries is used, but any combination of berries or other fruits will work. Peaches, plums, nectarines, and apples are all wonderful cobbler alternatives, but they will take a bit little longer to prep since they will need to be chopped into uniformly small pieces for even cooking. Make sure not to skip the lemon zest, since it nicely complements the sweetness of the berries. Serve this topped with Whipped Coconut Cream (page 121) or low-carb ice cream for an extra treat.

1. Preheat the oven to 325°F.

2. Spread the raspberries, blueberries, and black-berries out in an even layer in a 9-inch pie dish.

3. Sprinkle 2 tablespoons of sweetener over the berries.

4. In a medium bowl, combine the almond flour, coconut flour, remaining 2 tablespoons of sweet-ener, and the lemon zest. Mix well.

5. Add the egg, oil, and vanilla. Mix until a crumbly dough is formed.

6. Break off pieces of the dough over the berries, scattering them over the entire surface.

7. Transfer the dish to the oven and bake for 20 to 25 minutes, or until the top has lightly browned and the berries are bubbling. Remove from the oven. Serve warm.

Make it last: Store the cobbler in an airtight container in the refrigerator for up to 5 days.

PER SERVING: *Calories: 180; Total fat: 12g; Total carbohydrates: 13g; Fiber: 6g; Net carbs: 7g; Added sugar: 0g; Protein: 5g*

Honeycrisp Apple Galette

SERVES 8

PREP TIME: 15 minutes

COOK TIME: 50 minutes

1½ cups almond flour

2 tablespoons
coconut flour

1 large egg

1 tablespoon coconut oil

2 medium Honeycrisp
apples (about 3-inch
diameter), cored and
thinly sliced

¼ cup granulated
sweetener blend, plus
more for garnish

1 teaspoon freshly
squeezed lemon juice

1 teaspoon vanilla extract

½ teaspoon ground
cinnamon

Apple pie is comfort food sent straight from heaven, but it is often weighed down with copious amounts of sugar. Apples are rich in vitamin C, fiber, and antioxidants, making them a great addition to your healthy desserts. The recipe calls for Honeycrisps, but you can use any sweet variety; good options include Jonagold, Braeburn, Pink Lady, and Red Delicious. This rustic variation of pie requires no rolling, since it has a simple press-and-go almond flour crust on the bottom and no top crust. Arrange the apples in a circular or creative pattern for a lovely presentation.

1. Preheat the oven to 350°F.

2. To make the crust, in a medium bowl, mix together the almond flour and coconut flour.

3. Add the egg and oil. Form the mixture into a ball. Transfer to a 9-inch pie dish.

4. Using your hands or the bottom of a measuring cup, press the crust into the bottom of the dish and up the sides. Prick all over with a fork.

5. Transfer the dish to the oven and bake for 5 minutes. Remove from the oven, leaving the oven on. Let cool.

6. While the crust is cooking, in a medium bowl, combine the apples, sweetener, lemon juice, vanilla, and cinnamon. Toss to combine.

7. Arrange the apples in the pie dish in an even layer and press them gently into the crust, folding the sides in slightly over the apples.

8. Sprinkle lightly with sweetener to garnish.

9. Return the dish to the oven and bake for 30 minutes, or until the top has lightly browned.

10. Rotate the dish and bake for 15 more minutes, or until the apples are tender and the crust has browned. Remove from the oven. Let the galette cool for 15 minutes, then cut into 8 pieces.

Make it last: Store the galette in an airtight container in the refrigerator for up to 5 days.

PER SERVING: *Calories: 160; Total fat: 12g; Total carbohydrates: 11g; Fiber: 4g; Net carbs: 7g; Added sugar: 0g; Protein: 5g*

Coconut Cream Pie

SERVES 10

PREP TIME: 15 minutes, plus 2 hours to chill

COOK TIME: 20 minutes

2 cups shelled walnuts

¼ cup coconut oil

¼ cup granulated sweetener of choice

¼ cup arrowroot powder

3 cups milk of choice

1 cup unsweetened shredded coconut, plus more for garnish

1 teaspoon vanilla extract

1 cup Whipped Coconut Cream (page 121)

This light and creamy classic is typically loaded with sugar, but this elevated version is full of coconut flavor without the spike in blood sugar. Arrowroot powder is a nutrient-dense thickening agent that works with the shredded coconut to help set the pie. However, if you don't have any arrowroot, you can use cornstarch instead.

1. Preheat the oven to 350°F.

2. To make the crust, put the walnuts and oil in a food processor. Pulse until the walnuts are finely ground. Transfer to a 9-inch pie dish.

3. Using your hands or the bottom of a measuring cup, press the crust into the bottom of the dish and up the sides.

4. Transfer the dish to the oven and bake for 15 minutes, or until the top has lightly browned. Remove from the oven.

5. In a medium saucepan, mix together the sweetener and arrowroot.

6. Whisk in the milk slowly, then add the shredded coconut while stirring. Heat, stirring constantly, over medium heat, until the mixture boils. Remove from the heat.

7. Add the vanilla and mix well. Let cool for 15 minutes, then pour into the pie shell. Refrigerate for 2 hours to set and chill.

8. Top with the whipped coconut cream and sprinkle with shredded coconut to garnish, then serve.

PER SERVING: *Calories: 260; Total fat: 25g; Total carbohydrates: 5g; Fiber: 2g; Net carbs: 3g; Added sugar: 0g; Protein: 4g*

Strawberry Milkshake Pie

SERVES 8

PREP TIME: 15 minutes, plus 4 hours to chill

COOK TIME: 5 minutes

This strawberry and yogurt pie has a creamy milkshake feel and is very satisfying on a warm day. Gelatin holds the filling together and is necessary to help it set. Look for unflavored plain gelatin in the baking section of your grocery store. This pie is perfect when ripe strawberries are in season and at the peak of flavor, but it can just as easily be made with frozen strawberries.

FOR THE CRUST

1½ cups almond flour

1 tablespoon granulated sweetener blend

2 tablespoons coconut oil, melted

2 to 3 tablespoons cold water

FOR THE PIE

1½ cups chopped fresh or frozen strawberries

¼ cup water

2 teaspoons gelatin

1 cup plain low-fat Greek yogurt

½ cup powdered sweetener of choice

1 teaspoon vanilla extract

TO MAKE THE CRUST

1. In a medium bowl, whisk together the flour and sweetener.

2. Add the oil and mix well.

3. Drizzle in 2 tablespoons of water, then 1 more tablespoon, until the crust comes together.

4. Press the crust into a 9-inch pie dish, then transfer to the freezer.

TO MAKE THE PIE

5. Put a large bowl in the refrigerator to chill.

6. Put the strawberries and water in a blender. Puree. Transfer to a medium saucepan and bring to a simmer over low heat.

7. Slowly whisk in the gelatin. Remove from the heat. Let cool for about 20 minutes.

8. To make the filling, in the large, chilled bowl, combine the yogurt, powdered sweetener, and vanilla. Beat until combined.

9. Fold in the strawberry-gelatin mixture until mixed well.

10. Pour the cooled filling into the crust, and using a spatula, smooth the top. Refrigerate for at least 4 hours, or until the pie is firm and set.

Make it last: Store the pie covered in the refrigerator for up to 1 week.

PER SERVING: *Calories: 170; Total fat: 13g; Total carbohydrates: 7g; Fiber: 3g; Net carbs: 4g; Added sugar: 0g; Protein: 7g*

Classic Lemon Cream Pie

SERVES 8

PREP TIME: 20 minutes, plus 1 hour to chill

COOK TIME: 20 minutes

This lemon curd filling is made all the richer and more indulgent when combined with homemade Whipped Coconut Cream (page 121). The piecrust, made with just three simple ingredients, is a flaky, crisp crust that rivals a gluten crust any day. I like to use refined coconut oil when making this crust, since it creates a neutral flavor that is very versatile for both sweet and savory pies. However, if you are making a pie that would benefit from the coconut flavor of virgin coconut oil, such as this one, feel free to use it instead.

FOR THE CRUST

1½ cups almond flour

2 tablespoons coconut oil

2 to 3 tablespoons cold water

FOR THE PIE

½ cup coconut oil

½ cup granulated sweetener of choice

6 large egg yolks

½ cup freshly squeezed lemon juice

Zest of 2 lemons, minced or grated

1 recipe Whipped Coconut Cream (page 121)

TO MAKE THE CRUST

1. Preheat the oven to 350°F.

2. In a bowl, combine the almond flour, oil, and 2 tablespoons of water. Mix well until the crust holds together, adding up to 1 tablespoon more water as needed. Transfer to a 9-inch pie dish.

3. Using your hands or the bottom of a measuring cup, press the crust into the bottom of the dish and up the sides. Prick all over with a fork.

4. Transfer the dish to the oven and bake for 20 minutes, or until the crust is golden brown. Remove from the oven. Set aside to cool.

TO MAKE THE PIE

5. To make the filling, in a small pot, heat the oil and sweetener over medium heat until the sweetener has dissolved.

6. Add the egg yolks, lemon juice, and lemon zest. Whisk for 4 to 6 minutes, or until the curd just begins to thicken. Remove from the heat. Strain through a wire mesh strainer set over a large bowl. Use a spoon to help press the curd through the strainer. Set aside to cool.

7. Once cool, fold in the whipped coconut cream until well mixed.

8. Pour the filling into the piecrust and spread evenly. Refrigerate for 1 hour before serving.

Make it last: Store the piecrust in the refrigerator for up to 2 days before filling, or freeze for up to 6 months in an airtight container. Store the pie covered in the refrigerator for up 5 days.

PER SERVING: *Calories: 340; Total fat: 34g; Total carbohydrates: 5g; Fiber: 2g; Net carbs: 3g; Added sugar: 0g; Protein: 7g*

Pumpkin Pie

SERVES 10

PREP TIME: 15 minutes,
plus 2 hours to chill

COOK TIME: 55 minutes

FOR THE CRUST

1½ cups almond flour

2 tablespoons coconut oil

2 to 3 tablespoons
cold water

FOR THE PIE

1 (15-ounce) can plain
pumpkin puree

½ cup granulated
sweetener blend

1½ teaspoons pumpkin
pie spice

2 large eggs

1 cup milk of choice

1 teaspoon vanilla extract

Want to treat yourself with pumpkin pie, completely guilt-free? Do I have a recipe for you! By making your own pumpkin pie filling instead of using the canned version, you can easily cut down the sugar, keep the festive flavor, and completely upgrade the nutrient level. To keep it light, use a low-fat milk or your favorite unsweetened nut milk. If you don't have pumpkin pie spice, you can easily make your own by mixing together 1 teaspoon of ground cinnamon, ¼ teaspoon of ground ginger, and ¼ teaspoon of ground nutmeg. Serve topped with Whipped Coconut Cream (page 121), if desired.

TO MAKE THE CRUST

1. Preheat the oven to 350°F.

2. In a medium bowl, combine the flour, oil, and 2 tablespoons of water. Mix well until the crust holds together, adding up to 1 tablespoon more water as needed. Transfer to a 9-inch pie dish.

3. Using your hands or the bottom of a measuring cup, press the crust into the bottom of the dish and up the sides. Prick all over with a fork.

4. Transfer the dish to the oven and bake for 10 minutes, or until the top has lightly browned. Remove from the oven, leaving the oven on.

TO MAKE THE PIE

5. To make the filling, in a large bowl using a handheld electric mixer, blend the pumpkin puree, sweetener, pumpkin pie spice, and eggs on medium speed for 2 to 3 minutes, or until combined.

6. Reduce the speed to low. Mix in the milk and vanilla until smooth. Turn off the mixer. Pour the filling into the pie shell.

7. Return the dish to the oven and bake for 40 to 45 minutes, or until the filling is set. If the crust begins to brown too much before the filling is set, cover the crust with a ring of aluminum foil after about 30 minutes of baking. Remove from the oven. Let the pie cool to room temperature, then refrigerate for at least 2 hours, or until chilled and set.

Make it last: Store the pie covered in the refrigerator for up to 5 days.

PER SERVING: Calories: 190; Total fat: 14g; Total carbohydrates: 8g; Fiber: 4g; Net carbs: 4g; Added sugar: 0g; Protein: 6g

Grasshopper Pie

SERVES 10

PREP TIME: 20 minutes,
plus 2 hours to chill

COOK TIME: 20 minutes

FOR THE CRUST

1¼ cups almond flour

¼ cup unsweetened
cocoa powder

¼ teaspoon salt

2 tablespoons avocado oil

2 to 3 tablespoons water

FOR THE PIE

½ cup water

1 teaspoon plain gelatin

1 (8-ounce) package
low-fat cream cheese, at
room temperature

¾ cup powdered
sweetener of choice

1 teaspoon
peppermint extract

Pinch salt

1 cup heavy (whipping)
cream, cold

A favorite for its festive green color and its sweet and delightful mint essence, Grasshopper Pie is an absolute treat. The chocolaty rich black bottom crust is made from cocoa powder and almond flour, and the filling is light, sweet, and mint forward. If you would like to add the iconic grasshopper color, add a few drops of food-based natural green food coloring to the cream cheese in step 8. Or you can skip the color and just enjoy the great creamy texture and flavor.

TO MAKE THE CRUST

1. Preheat the oven to 350°F.

2. In a medium bowl, combine the flour, cocoa powder, and salt.

3. Add the oil and mix well.

4. Drizzle in the water, adding 2 tablespoons then 1 more tablespoon, until the crust comes together. Transfer to a 9-inch pie dish.

5. Using your hands or the bottom of a measuring cup, press the crust into the bottom of the dish and up the sides. Prick all over with a fork.

6. Transfer the dish to the oven and bake for 15 minutes, or until the crust has lightly browned. Remove from the oven. Cool the crust completely.

TO MAKE THE PIE

7.   Pour the water into a small saucepan and sprinkle the gelatin over the water. Heat over low heat, stirring, until the gelatin dissolves. Remove from the heat. Set aside to cool.

8.   In a large bowl using a handheld electric mixer, mix together the cream cheese, sweetener, peppermint extract, and salt on medium-high speed for 2 to 3 minutes, or until smooth. Turn off the mixer.

9.   In another bowl using a handheld electric mixer, beat the heavy cream on high speed for 4 to 5 minutes, or until soft peaks form. Turn off the mixer.

10. To make the filling, fold the whipped cream into the cream cheese mixture.

11. Stir the cooled gelatin into the mixture and mix until just combined.

12. Pour the filling into the piecrust, and using a spatula, smooth the top of the pie. Refrigerate for at least 2 hours, or until chilled and set.

Make it last: Store the pie covered for up to 5 days in the refrigerator.

PER SERVING: *Calories: 240; Total fat: 22g; Total carbohydrates: 6g; Fiber: 3g; Net carbs: 3g; Added sugar: 0g; Protein: 6g*

Black Bottom Peanut Butter and Chocolate Pie

SERVES 10

PREP TIME: 15 minutes, plus 2 hours to chill

COOK TIME: 10 minutes

If you love peanut butter and chocolate, you are going to *love* this black bottom pie that is stacked with a double layer of chocolate divinity. The peanut butter and cream cheese filling has the perfect level of sweet and savory and is sandwiched between a crumbly chocolate crust and a creamy chocolate coating. Be sure to use creamy peanut butter for this pie to add a subtle nutty flavor and to allow for an airy whipped mousse filling.

FOR THE CRUST

1 cup almond flour

2 tablespoons unsweetened cocoa powder

1 tablespoon coconut flour

1 tablespoon granulated sweetener of choice

2 tablespoons coconut oil

2 to 3 tablespoons water

FOR THE PIE

1 (8-ounce) package low-fat cream cheese, at room temperature

¼ cup creamy natural peanut butter

½ cup milk of choice

½ cup powdered sweetener of choice

2 teaspoons vanilla extract

½ cup no-sugar-added chocolate chips

2 teaspoons coconut oil

TO MAKE THE CRUST

1. Preheat the oven to 350°F.

2. In a medium bowl, combine the almond flour, cocoa powder, coconut flour, and granulated sweetener.

3. Drizzle in the oil and 2 tablespoons of water. Mix well until the crust holds together, adding up to 1 tablespoon more water as needed. Transfer to a 9-inch pie dish.

4. Using your hands or the bottom of a measuring cup, press the crust into the bottom of the dish and up the sides. Prick all over with a fork.

5. Transfer the dish to the oven and bake for 10 minutes, or until the crust has lightly browned. Remove from the oven. Set aside to cool.

TO MAKE THE PIE

6. To make the filling, in a large bowl using a hand-held electric mixer, beat the cream cheese and peanut butter on medium-high speed for 2 to 3 minutes, or until smooth.

7. Add the milk, powdered sweetener, and vanilla. Mix well until combined. Turn off the mixer.

8. Pour the filling into the cooled piecrust, and using a spatula, spread out evenly.

9. In a small microwave-safe bowl, combine the chocolate chips and oil. Microwave in 30-second intervals, stirring in between each interval, until melted and smooth.

10. Pour the chocolate over the filling to create an even layer on top. Chill for at least 2 hours before serving.

Make it last: Store the pie covered in the refrigerator for up to 1 week.

PER SERVING: Calories: 230; Total fat: 16g; Total carbohydrates: 10g; Fiber: 5g; Net carbs: 5g; Added sugar: 0g; Protein: 6g

Salted Caramel Pecan Pie

SERVES 10

PREP TIME: 30 minutes

COOK TIME: 1 hour
10 minutes

There is something magical that happens when you pair pecans with salted caramel. Brown sugar sweetener creates a nice caramel flavor, especially when coupled with coconut milk, which replaces butter for a healthier–and also very delicious–fat choice. This pie takes a little more time, since the coconut caramel needs to come to room temperature before making the filling, but the extra steps are well worth the final product.

FOR THE SALTED CARAMEL

2 cups full-fat coconut milk

¾ cup brown sweetener of choice

1 teaspoon vanilla extract

½ teaspoon salt

FOR THE CRUST

1½ cups almond flour

1 tablespoon granulated sweetener of choice

2 tablespoons coconut oil, melted

2 to 3 tablespoons cold water

FOR THE PIE

2 cups pecan halves, divided

1 teaspoon vanilla extract

½ teaspoon ground cinnamon

2 large eggs

TO MAKE THE SALTED CARAMEL

1. In a small pot, whisk together the coconut milk and brown sweetener. Bring to a simmer over medium heat.

2. Reduce the heat to low. Simmer, stirring regularly to avoid scorching, for 15 minutes, or until the mixture deepens in color to a darker brown. Remove from the heat.

3. Stir in the vanilla and salt. Set aside to cool to room temperature.

TO MAKE THE CRUST

4. Preheat the oven to 350°F.

5. In a medium bowl, whisk together the flour and granulated sweetener.

6. Add the oil and mix well.

7. Drizzle in the water, adding 2 tablespoons then 1 more tablespoon, until the crust comes together. Transfer to a 9-inch pie dish.

Continued ⟶

8. Using your hands or the bottom of a measuring cup, press the crust into the bottom of the dish and up the sides. Prick all over with a fork.

9. Transfer the dish to the oven and bake for 10 minutes. Remove from the oven. Let cool.

TO MAKE THE PIE

10. Chop 1½ cups of pecans and put in a medium bowl.

11. Add the vanilla and cinnamon. Mix well.

12. To make the filling, whisk the eggs one at a time into the pot of cooled salted caramel until the mixture is smooth. Fold into the pecan mixture.

13. Pour the filling into the crust, and arrange the remaining ½ cup of pecans over the top of the pie.

14. Transfer the dish to the oven and bake for 40 to 45 minutes, or until the center of the pie is set and the crust is golden brown. Remove from the oven. Cool completely to room temperature before serving.

Make it last: Store the pie covered in the refrigerator for up to 1 week.

PER SERVING: *Calories: 290; Total fat: 28g; Total carbohydrates: 6g; Fiber: 3g; Net carbs: 3g; Added sugar: 0g; Protein: 6g*

ALMOND BUTTERCREAM FROSTING, PAGE 123

Chapter 7

Divine Toppings

Berry Fruit Sauce

MAKES 1¼ CUPS

PREP TIME: 5 minutes

COOK TIME: 10 minutes

3 cups fresh or frozen mixed berries, such as blueberries, blackberries, raspberries

½ cup water

1 tablespoon granulated sweetener of choice

Pinch salt

This fruit sauce is great on Angel Food Cake (page 79) and is super quick and easy to make. Fresh or frozen berries work well in this sauce, and you can play around with other varieties based on what fruit you have available. The sauce thickens slightly when it cools, but if you prefer a thicker sauce, let it simmer for another few minutes to further reduce it.

1. In a small saucepan, combine the berries, water, sweetener, and salt. Bring to a simmer over medium heat. Cook for about 5 minutes, or until the berries are very soft and beginning to break down. Remove from the heat.

2. Using a fork or potato masher, smash the fruits into small pieces. Heat again over medium heat and simmer for about 2 minutes, or until the berries are well combined. Remove from the heat. Transfer to a storage container, let cool to room temperature, and refrigerate. The sauce will thicken slightly as it cools.

Make it last: Store the sauce in an airtight container in the refrigerator for up to 5 days.

PER SERVING (2 TABLESPOONS): *Calories: 20; Total fat: 0g; Total carbohydrates: 5g; Fiber: 2g; Net carbs: 3g; Added sugar: 0g; Protein: 0g*

Vanilla Glaze

MAKES ABOUT ¼ CUP

PREP TIME: 5 minutes

½ cup powdered sweetener of choice

2 tablespoons milk of choice

2 teaspoons coconut oil

1 teaspoon vanilla extract

This glaze is super versatile and can be drizzled over a variety of desserts to add a little extra sweetness and elegance. Drizzle it over Raspberry Oatmeal Bars (page 58) or Apple Pie Bars (page 54), or pair it with any favorite baked good. This makes a thin glaze that will drip down the sides of whatever you pour it on, which adds a nice gourmet touch. If you want something more spreadable, reduce the milk to 1 tablespoon.

1. In a small bowl, mix together the sweetener and milk, stirring to combine and break up any clumps.

2. Mix in the oil and vanilla. Continue mixing until smooth. Use immediately.

Make it last: Store the glaze in an airtight container in the refrigerator for up to 1 week, or freeze for up to 3 months.

PER SERVING (1 TABLESPOON): *Calories: 25; Total fat: 2.5g; Total carbohydrates: 0g; Fiber: 0g; Net carbs: 0g; Added sugar: 0g; Protein: 0g*

Whipped Coconut Cream

MAKES 1¼ CUPS

PREP TIME: 15 minutes

1 (13½-ounce) can full-fat coconut milk, chilled

¼ cup powdered sweetener of choice

Whipped Coconut Cream is a delicious dairy-free, no-sugar-added alternative to the store-bought version. To easily separate the coconut cream from the liquid in a can of coconut milk, be sure to refrigerate the entire can unopened overnight (or for at least 4 hours) for the best results. Look for coconut milk that does not have any fillers in it to ensure the cream and water separate in the can. Brands that work well include Aroy-D, 365 Whole Foods, and Native Forest coconut milk. Save the leftover coconut water for smoothies and other creamy beverages.

1. Chill a large mixing bowl for at least 10 minutes.

2. Without shaking or tipping the can, open the coconut milk. Leaving the liquid behind, spoon the thick coconut cream from the top of the can into the bowl.

3. Using a handheld electric mixer, beat the cream on medium speed for about 30 seconds or more, or until smooth.

4. Add the sweetener and mix for 30 seconds, or until smooth and creamy. Turn off the mixer. Use immediately or refrigerate until ready to use. The cream will harden further when chilled.

Make it last: Store the cream for up to 1 week in an airtight container in the refrigerator.

PER SERVING (1 TABLESPOON): *Calories: 30; Total fat: 3g; Total carbohydrates: 1g; Fiber: 0g; Net carbs: 1g; Added sugar: 0g; Protein: 0g*

Cream Cheese Frosting

MAKES ABOUT 1 CUP

PREP TIME: 5 minutes

1 (8-ounce) package low-fat cream cheese, at room temperature

2 tablespoons coconut oil

½ cup powdered sweetener of choice

½ teaspoon vanilla extract

This frosting is extremely versatile and pairs wonderfully with many of the desserts in this book. Low-fat cream cheese and coconut oil help make the frosting stiff and spreadable. Be sure to use powdered sweetener for the frosting for a smoother texture. If you don't have powdered sweetener on hand, you can process granulated sweetener in a blender for 30 seconds to 1 minute, or until it's a fine powder.

1. In a medium bowl using a handheld electric mixer, cream the cream cheese and oil on high speed for 2 to 3 minutes, or until smooth.

2. Add the powdered sweetener and vanilla. Mix well until combined. Turn off the mixer. Use immediately or store in an airtight container until you're ready to frost. Bring to room temperature before frosting.

Make it last: Store the frosting in an airtight container for up to 7 days in the refrigerator, or freeze for up to 3 months.

PER SERVING (1 TABLESPOON): *Calories: 45; Total fat: 4g; Total carbohydrates: 1g; Fiber: 0g; Net carbs: 1g; Added sugar: 0g; Protein: 1g*

Almond Buttercream Frosting

MAKES ⅔ CUP

PREP TIME: 5 minutes

½ cup no-sugar-added
  natural almond butter

2 tablespoons coconut oil

½ cup powdered
  sweetener of choice

½ teaspoon vanilla extract

Almond butter is a wonderful, thick base for frosting. Just four ingredients and a few minutes of blending yield a creamy, spreadable frosting that pairs well with most cakes. It is especially good on Triple Chocolate Cake (page 86) if you want to switch things up from the usual chocolate frosting on chocolate cake.

1. In a medium bowl using a handheld electric mixer, cream the almond butter and oil on high speed for 1 to 2 minutes, or until combined and smooth.

2. Add the powdered sweetener and vanilla. Mix until combined. Turn off the mixer. Use immediately or store in an airtight container until you're ready for frosting. Bring to room temperature before frosting.

Make it last: Store the frosting in an airtight container in the refrigerator for up to 1 week.

PER SERVING (2 TEASPOONS): *Calories: 90; Total fat: 8g; Total carbohydrates: 2g; Fiber: 1g; Net carbs: 1g; Added sugar: 0g; Protein: 3g*

Measurement Conversions

VOLUME EQUIVALENTS	U.S. STANDARD	U.S. STANDARD (OUNCES)	METRIC (APPROXIMATE)
LIQUID	2 tablespoons	1 fl. oz.	30 mL
	¼ cup	2 fl. oz.	60 mL
	½ cup	4 fl. oz.	120 mL
	1 cup	8 fl. oz.	240 mL
	1½ cups	12 fl. oz.	355 mL
	2 cups or 1 pint	16 fl. oz.	475 mL
	4 cups or 1 quart	32 fl. oz.	1 L
	1 gallon	128 fl. oz.	4 L
DRY	⅛ teaspoon	–	0.5 mL
	¼ teaspoon	–	1 mL
	½ teaspoon	–	2 mL
	¾ teaspoon	–	4 mL
	1 teaspoon	–	5 mL
	1 tablespoon	–	15 mL
	¼ cup	–	59 mL
	⅓ cup	–	79 mL
	½ cup	–	118 mL
	⅔ cup	–	156 mL
	¾ cup	–	177 mL
	1 cup	–	235 mL
	2 cups or 1 pint	–	475 mL
	3 cups	–	700 mL
	4 cups or 1 quart	–	1 L
	½ gallon	–	2 L
	1 gallon	–	4 L

OVEN TEMPERATURES

FAHRENHEIT	CELSIUS (APPROXIMATE)
250°F	120°C
300°F	150°C
325°F	165°C
350°F	180°C
375°F	190°C
400°F	200°C
425°F	220°C
450°F	230°C

WEIGHT EQUIVALENTS

U.S. STANDARD	METRIC (APPROXIMATE)
½ ounce	15 g
1 ounce	30 g
2 ounces	60 g
4 ounces	115 g
8 ounces	225 g
12 ounces	340 g
16 ounces or 1 pound	455 g

Index

• Acknowledgments •

There are many people who have impacted me more than they will ever know. On the top of that list is the love of my life, my husband, Jace Warren. Through the years he has always encouraged and supported me, but because of his hardworking nature, he continually motivates me to do better and to work harder. I want to thank my little stinkers: Barrett, Zona, and the little one kicking inside while writing this book. They are my daily motivation to manage my diabetes well. I want to thank my loving parents, Mark and Carol Barratt, for their guidance, dedication, and for many wonderful and happy memories. I want to thank my in-laws, Kelly and Scott Warren, whom I regard as my best friends. I want to thank my dear friend, AnneMarie Rousseau, who also has diabetes and has dedicated her life as a diabetes health-care professional. I want to thank the very talented editor Lauren Ladoceour for seeking me out as a writer and sticking with me for the past two books. Lastly, to all my friends out there who have diabetes, I see you as my comrades. We are in this together. From the bottom of my heart, *thank you*.

• About the Author •

 Ariel Warren is a registered dietitian nutritionist (RDN) and a Certified Diabetes Care and Education Specialist (CDCES). She was diagnosed with type 1 diabetes at the age of four in 1995, which has served as her primary motivator to pursue a career in health care as an educator. Ariel graduated from Brigham Young University in nutrition and dietetics with her bachelor's, then completed her dietetic internship as Utah State University. She then spent several years as a diabetes educator working at a local outpatient endocrinology clinic. Today, Ariel works as a health-care provider through her online private practice, where she helps people improve their diabetes management through nutrition and lifestyle choices. She gives back to the community by writing diabetes education books and articles, speaking on optimizing control through tech and nutrition, creating education videos, building an online diabetes website and community with her husband, and by serving those in her community through organizations such as the Association of Diabetes Care and Education Specialists (ADCES). Ariel loves empowering people with diabetes through food and lifestyle choices so they can live long and healthy lives.